COLLECTING STAMPS
FOR PLEASURE
& PROFIT

BARRY KRAUSE

BETTERWAY PUBLICATIONS, INC.
WHITE HALL, VIRGINIA

Published by Betterway Publications, Inc.
Box 219
Crozet, VA 22932

Cover design by Deborah Chappell

Photography by Marlene Wallace of Los Angeles, California.
All stamps photographed from the stock of Superior Stamp
& Coin Company, Beverly Hills, California.

All stamp catalog numbers are from Scott Publishing Company, Sidney, Ohio.

Library of Congress Cataloging-in-Publication Data

Collecting stamps for pleasure and profit
  p. cm
Includes index.
ISBN 1-558-70105-2 (pbk.) : $8.95
1. Postage-stamps--Collectors and collecting.   I. Title.
HE6215.K72 1988   88-19413
769.56'075--dc19   CIP

Printed in the United States of America
0987654321

To young stamp collectors of the world.
Happy are the children who have
a precious hobby like stamp collecting,
for they have two worlds to live in instead of one!

ACKNOWLEDGMENTS

Without these people in my life, this book might not be here:

Paul McCallum — the inspiration for it all, who suggested that I write a stamp book before I tackle my more ambitious projects!

Steve Joyner — who arranged all the photography sessions and helped with "Federal Expressing" the manuscript.

Peter Linde, Jay O'Donnell, and Paul Arenson — who reminded me to continue with the book when I was distracted.

Leonard J. Krause and Helen Krause — my parents, who gave me the best foundation a writer can have: a happy childhood.

Superior Stamp & Coin Company, Beverly Hills, California — who generously allowed me to photograph their stamps.

Marlene Wallace of Los Angeles, California — for photographing the stamps.

My grade school and high school teachers — who taught me how to write.

My students (past and present) — who keep me young and hopeful.

My uncle — who gave me my first stamp album and opened up a door that I never knew existed until then.

The staff of Betterway Publications, Inc. — whose editing, production, and business procedures make me proud to be one of their authors.

ABOUT THE STAMPS ON THE FRONT COVER

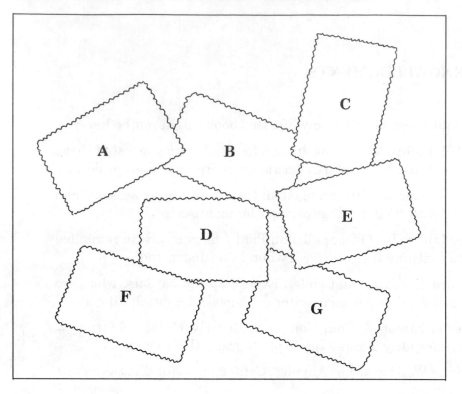

A. Wright Brothers air mail 6-cent issued to commemorate the 46th anniversary of powered flight on Dec. 17, 1945. Scott #C45.

B. Red Cross 3-cent commemorative of Nov. 21, 1952, issued to honor the International Red Cross in 1864. Scott #1016.

C. Byrd Antarctic 3-cent commemorative of Oct. 9, 1933, issued in conjunction with the Byrd Antarctic Expedition of 1933 for use on mail cancelled at the Little America Post Office, Antarctica. Scott #733 and varieties.

D. California 3-cent stamp issued to commemorate the 100th anniversary of the admission of California to the Union: Sept. 9, 1950. Scott #977.

E. 6-cent air mail issue of May 14, 1938 with vignette of "Eagle Holding Shield, Olive Branch, and Arrows." Scott #C23.

F. Moon Landing 10-cent air mail issued Sept. 9, 1969 to honor the first manned moon landing which was on July 20, 1969. Scott #C76.

G. Lewis and Clark Expedition 3-cent commemorative issued on July 28, 1954 for the 150th anniversary of the start of the famous Lewis and Clark Expedition which explored the Louisiana Purchase. Scott #1063.

Contents

Introduction

Why stamps?

Because they're beautiful, historical, and available little works of art. Because they're so much a part of our lives, every time we turn to the mailbox. Because they're valuable. Because they're a ticket to a world of vicarious and real adventure, a wonderland of the heights and depths where human dreams and fantasies play out their drama via government postal paper.

Because stamps are ambassadors from distant lands, teachers of geography and civics, messengers from the minds and souls of past and present people. Because stamps chart the rise and fall of nations and individuals, a paper record of the pageantry of nineteenth and twentieth century civilization.

Who hasn't glanced with burning curiosity at the exotic postage stamp on a foreign letter? Or guessed at the possibilities of what's inside a mysterious envelope covered with a dozen different colorful adhesives? Or lifted a brittle fading message out of its household tomb of forgotten family correspondence, testimony of once-important mail stamped and sent by the enthusiastic ghosts of another time and place?

Why stamps? Because they're fun, sometimes financially profitable, always a joy to behold and study, and often a source of endless entertainment in your spare hours. And you can collect stamps alone or in a crowd, doing business in person or by mail with distant philatelists you will never see.

Imagine a lifetime of idle moments squandered with trivial diversions, with lingering regrets of missed opportunities, and vaguely dissolving memories of quickly lost cheap thrills. *Then* imagine a lifetime with free hours devoted to a hobby that draws the best of you from within, and fills the pauses in your days and nights with real information and the satisfaction of knowing something worthwhile. Imagine having exciting moments to look forward to, when other things aren't occupying your thoughts and acts. Imagine waking up when you're old with some of the same feelings of anticipation and wonder that you had when you were young.

Imagine being a stamp collector!

Chapter 1

Collecting, Accumulating, or Investing

WHY WE COLLECT — Collecting is instinctive in human beings. From the time we are little children we have an inner drive to admire and acquire nonessential things.

Five year old children walk along the beach, filling their pockets with pretty stones and seashells. Junior high school students collect rock music recordings, clothes and posters in the latest styles, photos of their families and friends, school yearbooks, stuffed toy animals, baseball cards, and model airplanes.

Adults collect antique furniture, art, rare books, movie memorabilia, Indian artifacts, war souvenirs, and classic cars if they have money. Family scrapbooks, grocery store coupons, old love and business letters saved for their memories, favorite tools, and trinkets purchased during travels are the heirlooms of the middle class. Cheap costume jewelry, old magazines, used dishes, and miscellaneous junk are the collections of the less well-to-do.

Why do we collect? It gives us a sense of order in what might be otherwise confusing lives. By finding, cleaning, arranging, and showing off interesting and unusual objects, we gain a feeling of control and predictability in the face of daily uncertainties.

We collect because we want to show off our treasures to other people, to make profits from wise collecting investments, to learn about the items that fascinate us, and to experience the thrill of the chase in tracking down and recognizing choice additions to our collections. Collecting gives us an excuse to socialize with fellow enthusiasts, to join clubs and societies in our field of specialty, and to gain the respect and awe of those who aren't as lucky or as smart as we are in obtaining and appreciating the material things that make up our exhibit.

For kids with growing pains and school pressures, and for adults with boring or tense jobs, collecting is an escape into a manageable world that curiously borders between fantasy and reality. If you've just had a bad day, you can come home and play with your dolls or Ming vases. You can't control the ten o'clock news, but you can line up your buttons and marbles, curl up in bed with the latest auction catalogs and price lists, and dream about stumbling on that dusty attic filled with wonderful objects waiting for your magic touch.

THE FIRST STAMPS

And so we come to stamp collecting. Coins are older, rare autographs and old manuscripts more traditional, and high tech modern art more immediate, but stamps provide a source of wonder and satisfaction that is hard to match in other collecting hobbies.

The first adhesive postage was Great Britain's famous "Penny Black," first issued by the British Post Office on May 6, 1840. Current catalog value (Scott's) is $3,500 for a mint copy, $200 for a cancelled version, and a pristine example with wide margins would sell at retail or auction for close to those prices.

Almost from the start, people began to save postage stamps. In the 1840s, a young lady placed an advertisement in a London newspaper, asking for donations of the new stamps to paper the walls of her room. Some philatelic scholars have suggested that this ad was really placed by one of the first stamp dealers, hoping to get free stamps for his business.

Other countries followed Britain's lead in introducing stamps to their citizens. On February 1, 1842, Alexander M. Greig and Henry Thomas Windsor started the New York City Despatch Post, a local postal service in Manhattan. They issued their own stamps showing a full face view of George Washington surrounded by the words, "CITY DESPATCH POST, THREE CENTS." Printed in engraved black ink on grayish paper by the New York City firm of Rawdon, Wright & Hatch, this was the first adhesive stamp used in the United States, and now catalogs at $300 mint, $150 used.

The first government outside of Great Britain to produce stamps was the canton of Zurich, Switzerland which issued Four Rappen and Six Rappen stamps (100 Rappen equalled one Franc) on March 1, 1843. Brazil joined the world's stamp manufacturing fraternity on August 1, 1843.

On July 1, 1847 the first nationwide, postally valid United States stamps were released, the classic U.S. issues so popular among philatelists and stamp investors, the five cent Franklin ($4,500 mint, $700 used) red-brown on thin bluish wove paper, and the ten cent Washington black ink on the same bluish paper ($18,500 mint, $2,000 used).

1. Five cent New York City Postmaster Provisional issued imperforate. Earliest known use July 15, 1845. Catalog value $325 used. Catalog #9X1.

2. Five cent Franklin and ten cent Washington, the first regular U.S. stamps, issued July 1, 1847. Catalog value $700 and $2000, respectively, in cancelled condition. Catalog #1 and #2.

4. Five cent Franklin on cover. U.S. catalog #1 on cover. Red circular date stamp (CDS) probably New York City, addressed to Utica, New York. Nice four-margined copy of the first regular U.S. stamp. Catalog value $850 on cover.

3. Great Britain's Penny Black, the world's first postage stamp, issued May 6, 1840. Imperforated black ink on white paper, small crown watermark. Catalog value $3500 mint, $200 used. Catalog #Great Britain 1.

The first stamps approved for a British colonial government were the one penny orange and two penny dark blue "Post Office" Mauritius issues of September 21, 1847. Mauritius is an island in the Indian Ocean about 550 miles east of Madagascar. The capital is Port Louis where James Barnard, a jeweler with failing eyesight, was living in 1847. Because he was a watchmaker and engraver, it was decided that Barnard would design the island's first stamps.

But he apparently forgot his instructions for the wording on the stamps, and instead of engraving "POST PAID" to the left of Queen Victoria's portrait, he put "POST OFFICE." Legend says that as he was walking home he noticed the words "Post Office" on the front of the Port Louis Post Office. Being familiar with the handstamps saying "Post Office Mauritius," used at that time to strike postal markings on the island's pre-stamp era mail, he decided that "POST OFFICE" were the two words that belonged on the stamp's left border.

Of the 500 stamps of each denomination produced, only a couple of dozen total copies have been discovered to date. The rare "POST OFFICE" Mauritius stamps catalog $500,000 mint and $350,000 used for either the one penny or two penny values.

The first Asian stamps were the Indian district of Scinde issues (July 1, 1852), and the first African stamps were the Cape of Good Hope triangulars of September 1, 1853. By the 1860s, most civilized countries were using stamps on their mail.

THE FIRST DEALERS

Stamp dealers sprang up to cater to the needs of mid-nineteenth century fledgling collectors. Moens in Belgium, Gibbons in England, and Scott in the United States pioneered and set the foundation of stamp dealing as we know it today.

Jean-Baptiste Moens started selling stamps in his Brussels bookshop in 1848. Some researchers claim it was 1852. Moens also published useful books, catalogs, and pamphlets related to stamp collecting.

Edward Stanley Gibbons was born in 1840, the same year as the birth of the world's first postage stamp, Britain's Penny Black. He claimed to be a stamp dealer at age sixteen, and by 1874 he moved his store to London where it still exists as the oldest stamp company in the world. The Gibbons stamp catalogs are the oldest in continuous publication, begun by Gibbons in 1865.

Gibbons made stamp collecting a respectable pastime and was responsible for some spectacular finds. One occurred the day a couple of sailors entered his shop and dumped a huge sack of rare Cape of Good Hope triangular stamps (the first issues of that colony) on his counter. They said they got the stamps somewhere in South Africa, and Gibbons gladly purchased them, probably at a dirt cheap price for what today would be a classic stamp hoard worth a veritable fortune!

J. Walter Scott began producing stamp catalogs in the United States in 1867 and 1868. Born in England, he came to America and became our country's most well-known stamp dealer. The Scott Publishing Company which produces catalogs and albums at the present is the recognized authority on stamp catalog listings in the United States. Scott Publishing Company, located in Sidney, Ohio, is a direct business descendant of J. Walter Scott's firm which has undergone many changes of ownership in the last hundred years.

ACCUMULATING STAMPS

An accumulator is a person who likes to get more and more of something. The accumulation may grow to unmanageable proportions, outstripping the space limitations and storage facilities available.

A stamp accumulator starts out by saving sheets (panes) of stamps as they are issued by the local post office. He or she may clip stamps off the envelopes of incoming mail, and often asks friends and relatives to save stamps for this "collection."

But it isn't really a collection because it has no form or direction. Many individuals call themselves stamp collectors when in fact they are mere accumulators of mint, cancelled, and on-cover stamps. An accumulation of covers may be all mixed up in a shoe box, unsorted, unstudied, and to a large extent unappreciated. An accumulation of stacks and stacks of mint commemorative sheets and bags of cancelled stamps can gather dust for years while their owner is always intending to organize it, but never does.

A typical accumulator has a little of everything and not an in-depth representation of anything. First day covers out of sequence, a glassine envelope filled with miscellaneous plate number blocks, and cigar boxes of foreign pictorials are what make up the stamp life of the accumulator.

An accumulator is usually not a member of any stamp club or society, doesn't subscribe to any philatelic publications, and doesn't particularly care about the money value of the stamps. He visits stamp dealers irregularly, usually to spend pocket change on cheap stamps and covers selected on impulse, without thought to a long-range collecting plan.

Many stamp collectors begin their hobby as accumulators, and there is nothing wrong in dabbling with stamps for light entertainment and momentary diversion. But you must realize that your accumulation is not a coherent collection, and will probably never be of great interest to a serious collector or dealer, and therefore probably never be of great money value.

It is pleasant to spend a rainy day soaking stamps off their envelopes, or spreading out a box of old covers on the kitchen table to look at their postmarks for the thirtieth time.

COLLECTING STAMPS

A stamp collector has goals, order, logic, and realistic tactics in the acquisition and use of stamps. Unlike the mere accumulator, the collector often has albums of one country or the world, with spaces for each nation's stamps in chronological arrangement. The true collector reads books and periodicals about stamps.

You may graduate into collecting from first accumulating unrelated groups of stamps and covers, gradually realizing that certain of your stamps (maybe airmails or postage dues or animal topicals) interest you more than others. Or you could decide to specialize in one country's stamps or the issues from a particular time period (like World War II covers or stamps of the world issued during your birth year).

A collector studies the stamps that he or she owns. Collectors make plans as to the future direction that the collection will take, given enough time and money.

A collector subscribes to dealer price lists and stamp auction catalogs, and submits bids and want lists for needed items. Within the limits of finances, a collector is much more willing to spend cash for more stamps, instead of hoping that more will come his way for little or no cost.

Collectors are aware of market prices, including the normal spread between wholesale and retail values of often-traded issues. A collector considers future potential profits when buying stamps, but will also buy an item because it fits the collection, regardless of price.

When a stamp collector undertakes serious study of a stamp series and contributes original research about those stamps, then a philatelist is born. The philatelist is the most knowledgeable collector, well-read in a field of stamp specialization. He has spent much time (and maybe funds!) examining stamps, and is in a position to make authoritative comments about them.

A collector needs a full range of stamp equipment to pursue an intelligent collection: stamp catalogs, specialized books, stamp tongs, watermarking tray and fluid, color comparison charts, perforation gauges, and proper albums and protective mounts are normally found at the collector's desk. The stamp accumulator is often ignorant of these collecting tools.

INVESTING IN STAMPS

Probably most people who think they are stamp investors are actually stamp speculators. A commodity speculator hopes for profits within a year or two. A genuine stamp investor thinks about the long term price performance of selected rare stamp issues, preferring to wait five or ten years to turn a decent profit rather than risk disappointment by trying for a "quick kill" in the short run.

The wisest investors are collectors first and investors second. Only by taking time to learn about stamps can you insure that you will have a chance in making profitable investment decisions in philately.

While it is true that stamps that are admired by collectors often make sound investments, the investor must make investment decisions based on market analysis and not on aesthetic factors alone. In other words, a stamp bought for investment should be bought with profits in mind regardless of whether or not the investor emotionally likes or dislikes the particular issue.

Many modern topicals from Communist countries are close to worthless in market value because they are printed in large quantities for a saturated market. On the other hand, stamps that are not especially beautiful (like the one cent British Guiana of 1856, last auctioned off for close to $1,000,000) may be superb long-term investments.

In Chapter 8 we'll look closely at the rules of intelligent stamp investing, as well as identifying particular stamps that have performed well in the market over the past fifteen years, and have potential for similar price growth during the rest of this century.

Many collectors divide their stamps into all three of the categories we've been examining: those stamps of marginal value accumulated for their entertainment use, stamps bought for building a logical collection (like an album of Confederate covers or all mint issues of France since 1940), and stamps acquired for investment (like Zeppelin sets or the early Israeli coin stamps of 1948 with full tabs attached).

Chapter 2

Basic Collecting Tools

Collecting stamps without the proper tools is like going to war without weapons or armor. Sure, you can get by with envelopes or shoe boxes full of stamps, but when you start buying more expensive items or delicate, poorly preserved stamps and covers, you will wish you had *collecting accessories*, as they are known.

Also, many stamps are impossible to identify without watermarking fluid or perforation measurements, and repairs or faked stamps can be more easily detected with simple standard philatelic tools. Then, too, you don't want to damage your stamps, and the proper tools will enable you to handle the most expensive item with a minimum of risk of injuring it.

STAMP TONGS Because paper is fragile and hard to pick up without altering it by bending, getting it dirty, etc., stamp tongs were invented for the safe handling of philatelic material. Tongs look a lot like medical tweezers, with the exception of the gripping inside surfaces of the tips: first aid tweezers are usually roughened or serrated, stamp tongs are always flat and smooth. Never use medical tweezers to pick up stamps because the roughened edges might dig into the paper and damage it.

The best tongs are made of stainless steel. Luxurious ones are available gold-plated or custom engraved with the owner's initials. Inexpensive nickel tongs are okay for beginners who will eventually graduate to better ones if they stay in philately.

Tongs are called a "pair" even though they are a single device (like a pair of scissors). So when you ask to use a dealer's tongs to look at one of his stamps, ask for a pair of tongs, not a tong.

The shape of the tips varies, depending on an individual's preference and expertise in using tongs. Beginners generally do better with wide tips which are good for gripping a stamp no matter where you grab it. Dealers and advanced philatelists normally prefer narrow-pointed tongs which can be easily slid underneath the thinnest stamp, and don't hide much of the stamp's surface when it is being held in the tongs. Some point styles are:

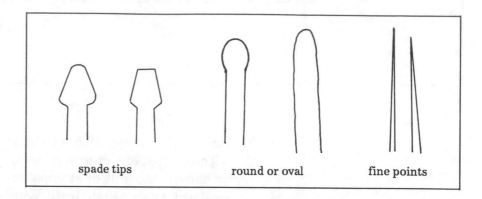

spade tips   round or oval   fine points

Stamp tongs cost between $2 and $5 for the cheaper varieties, $5 to $10 for the better ones. A beginner should buy the cheapest tongs. Expensive fine-pointed tongs can puncture a stamp if improperly used; stamp collecting and philatelic investing require patience. If you need to be an expert at once, try video games or frisbee tossing.

STAMP HINGES

Stamp hinges became popular in the early twentieth century as they replaced the glue and homemade hinges of stamp collectors in the 1800s. A stamp hinge is a tiny piece of glassine translucent paper (something like kitchen waxed paper, but thinner), usually light green or gray in color, with one side gummed for sticking to stamps and album pages.

Hinges come flat and prefolded, rectangular with sharp corners or with gently rounded corners:

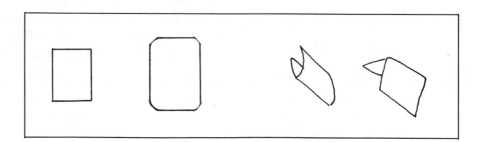

To mount a stamp with a hinge on an album page, use a prefolded hinge or fold one of the flat types so that the gummed side faces outward. Lightly moisten one half of the gummed side of the hinge with your tongue and, holding the hinge with a stamp tongs, press the moistened side against the top back of a stamp lying face down on the table:

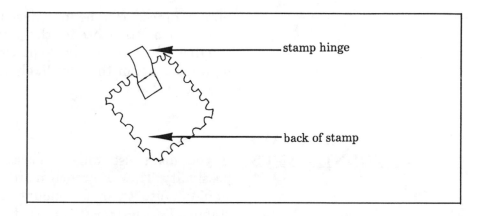

Then fold the hinge flat against the stamp and moisten the other part of the hinge and mount it at the proper place in your album. If you make a mistake and mount the stamp in the wrong place, wait a day for the hinge to become thoroughly dry before trying to lift it off the page; otherwise you could tear and damage the stamp with a still moist hinge adhering to the stamp's paper.

The whole purpose of hinges is to keep your stamps conveniently arranged on album pages, without going to the trouble of having complicated plastic mounts. A hinge also allows you to lift up a stamp already mounted on an album page, and inspect its reverse side without removing it from the page:

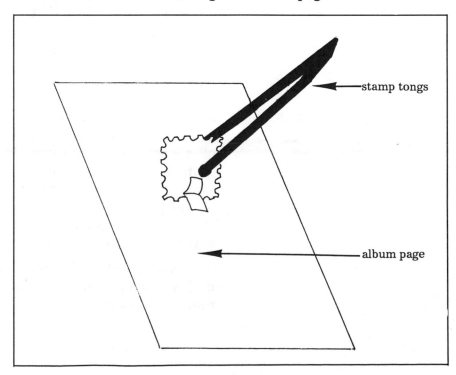

Stamp hinges can be purchased for about $1.50 to $2 per thousand, a little more for the prefolded type. Like all philatelic supplies, they should be kept clean and away from heat and high humidity or they are likely to curl or stick together in the opened package.

OTHER WAYS TO MOUNT STAMPS

If you don't use hinges, plastic mounts and sleeves are a possibility. They are much more expensive than hinges, so you wouldn't use them for mounting a large collection of cheap stamps. Furthermore, stamps are hard to sell in plastic mounts because the dealer doesn't like the time-consuming task of removing each stamp from its mount to check it for defects.

My recommendation is to use plastic mounts for more valuable stamps, leaving one side open to the air so that your stamp can "breathe." Do consider what your album will look like if you use a lot of mounts in it: maybe a bit too bulky due to the "thickening" effect that plastic protective stamp mounts have on stacked album pages.

Mounts are manufactured in a variety of plastics ranging from Mylar to acetates. Manufacturers and dealers are hesitant to guarantee that your stamps won't be harmed by a particular brand of mount, so you have to take your chances. But regular inspections and "airing out" of your collection by turning the pages now and then should alert you to chemical damage or other problems (like stamp curling, gum of mint stamps sticking to the mounts) before your whole collection is destroyed.

ALBUMS

Perhaps the easiest method for mounting and keeping stamps in order is to use a stock book with glassine, cardboard, or plastic pockets on the pages. Some printed albums for particular countries have pictures of the stamps arranged in chronological, catalog number order, with plastic pocket mounts glued on top of the picture which shows through the clear mount. Blank stock books are available in many sizes from small pocket or safe deposit box dimensions to large 8-1/2 x 11 inch pages or bigger.

An advantage of stock books over hinged or individually plastic-mounted stamps is that stamps in a stock book are simple to remove or rearrange:

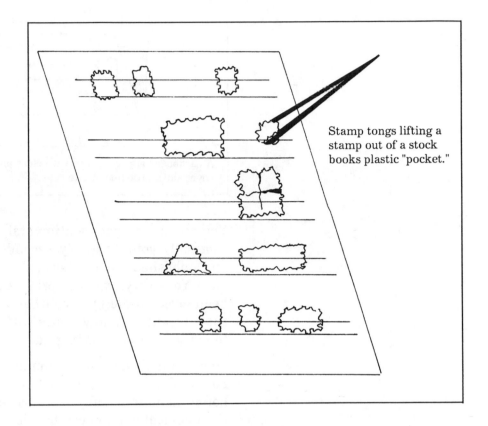

Stamp tongs lifting a
stamp out of a stock
books plastic "pocket."

It is hard to find a good $10 album any more, and even
beginners might be wise to invest $20 or $30 in a stamp album.
A more expensive album won't fill up too quickly, making the
purchase of a larger one necessary, followed by many hours
transferring stamps from the smaller to larger album.

Any stamp shop will be happy to show you a selection of albums
in your price range. They may even have a few used ones lying
around, at a big discount off retail price.

Get an album that fits your collecting goals. If you know nothing
about stamps and are a beginner in the hobby, try a cheap
worldwide album with a small packet of foreign stamps to
practice identifying and mounting with hinges. If you know that
your interests are specialized and more narrow, maybe a single
country album (such as Germany or Mexico) is for you. If you're
an investor, get a stock book or plastic approval cards that will
fit into your safe deposit box at the bank.

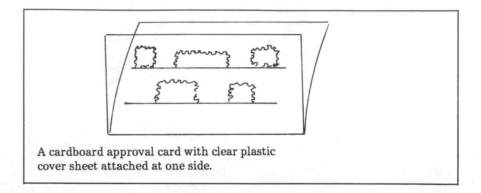

A cardboard approval card with clear plastic cover sheet attached at one side.

You tend to get sentimental about your stamp albums, especially your first. My second album, titled the "Aristocrat" and published by, I believe, the Grossman Stamp Company of New York City, was my pride and joy for many years, having been given to me by my father when I was a little boy. I think that I spent as many hours with this album as I did watching television when I was in grade school!

One more thing about albums: they come either completely bound like a hardcover book or in looseleaf binder format. The bound albums usually have pages that are easier to turn, but the looseleaf version can be added to with yearly supplements if you are collecting current stamps of a country.

The most popular albums in any country are those specializing in that country's stamps. Albums for U.S. stamps alone have heavy sales in the United States, while Great Britain or British colonial albums sell well in the British Isles. Most collectors save stamps of their native country before they specialize in a foreign nation's philately.

PERFORATION GAUGES   The number of "holes" or "teeth" that are on two centimeters (2 cm.) of the length of a stamp's side is that stamp's perforation gauge number. For example, if there are ten perforation holes in two centimeters of stamp edge, the stamp is called *Perf. 10*. Some stamps have a different perforation number for their horizontal side as compared with their vertical edge.

Many stamps with identical designs and colors have been issued with different perforation numbers, so the serious collector must own a perforation gauge device in order to distinguish which perforation type a stamp happens to be.

Perforation gauges are made of metal, cardboard, or clear plastic, and usually measure about 5 x 2 inches. They have printed on their surfaces the most likely encountered perforation numbers in dots or spaces, with the appropriate gauge number next to the row:

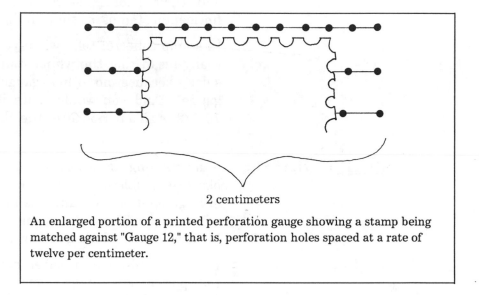

2 centimeters

An enlarged portion of a printed perforation gauge showing a stamp being matched against "Gauge 12," that is, perforation holes spaced at a rate of twelve per centimeter.

As shown in the drawing, stamp perforation numbers can be fractions, like 11-1/2 or 8-1/2. Also, remember that a stamp doesn't know what its gauge is supposed to be. Stamp paper that has expanded or shrunk over the years, errors in precision gauge manufacture, and production mistakes in giving a stamp the wrong gauge may make you think a given stamp is a different variety than what it in fact is.

Compound perforations exist when the horizontal (top and bottom sides) perforation number is different from the vertical number. In this case, we customarily give the horizontal gauge first, then the vertical: perforated 11 x 10-1/2, or 14 x 14-1/2.

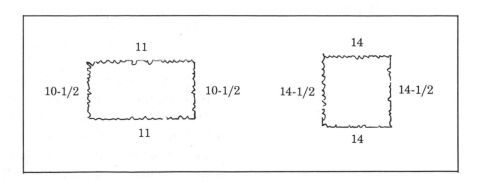

United States stamps from the Civil War to 1912 were perforated with a gauge of 12. In the 1920s and 1930s, perf. 11 was popular for U.S. issues, and later commemoratives of the 1940s and 1950s typically had their longer dimensions perf. 11 and their shorter sides perf. 10-1/2 (or 11 x 10-1/2 for horizontal stamps, as they are indicated in the catalogs).

In stamp collector talk, when you say "perf ten and a half," you really mean that the whole stamp has a gauge of 10-1/2 on all sides (because no other gauge was stated as a "compound gauge"). And you would write it in shorthand like this: *Perf. 10-1/2*, with a period after the abbreviation for *perforated*.

MAGNIFYING GLASSES

A magnifying glass helps you to see fine details on a stamp: obscure portions of the intricately engraved design, an enlargement of the numerals in a cancellation, or the structure of the paper fibers of a suspicious looking edge that may have been repaired to hide a tear or thin spot.

I recommend a two or three power lens for average use, and a ten power lens (like a jeweler's loupe) for extremely fine "blowups," looking at the stamps of course with adequate light coming from the side (not through the top of the magnifier).

Stamp dealers sell a variety of magnifiers in prices ranging from a couple of dollars to $15 or more. Any magnifying glass is okay for beginners, and you probably won't use it as much as you think you will unless you start buying expensive stamps or investing serious money in a stamp portfolio.

And if you're holding a stamp in tongs under the magnifier, be careful to do this over a table so that if the stamp falls from the tongs it won't float to the floor and pick up dirt.

WATERMARKING FLUID AND TRAY

Watermarks are security measures impressed on stamp paper during its manufacture to inhibit counterfeiting. A watermark is a specific design which appears as a thin spot on the stamp when held up to the light. The watermark may be letters like USPS for United States Postal Service, or a crown for British Empire issues, or just a series of wavy lines. The stamp catalogs illustrate watermarks and tell which stamps have them and which don't — a vital bit of information because some stamps of identical design are worth more with (or without) the watermark, compared to the more common variety.

With a small bottle of watermarking fluid (say, four ounces) and a black plastic watermark tray you can detect watermarks more accurately than by merely squinting at a stamp held up to the light.

Place a stamp face down in the tray (usually measuring a few inches in a rectangular shape by half an inch deep), put a little watermark fluid over the stamp, and if a watermark is present it should show up against the tray as an area darker than the unwatermarked portions of the stamp paper:

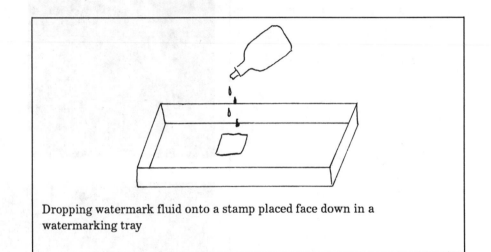

Dropping watermark fluid onto a stamp placed face down in a watermarking tray

Watermarking fluids are organic compounds that are harmless to most stamps. The fluid evaporates quickly, leaving the stamp undamaged, even if it has gum on the back. Never put a gummed stamp in water unless you want to wash off all the gum.

Some watermarking fluids are flammable. Some are toxic if their vapors are inhaled in sufficient amounts. Read the directions on the bottle, and always use watermarking fluid with good ventilation, preferably next to an open window. I once tried watermarking a group of stamps near a fan for safer air circulation, and blew dozens of stamps all over the room!

And don't forget that when a stamp is wet with watermark fluid it should be handled carefully so that it doesn't tear. Put stamps into, and lift them out of watermark trays with stamp tongs. I like to hold a stamp that has been tested up in the air for a few seconds to allow excess watermark fluid to evaporate, which it does readily, being highly volatile.

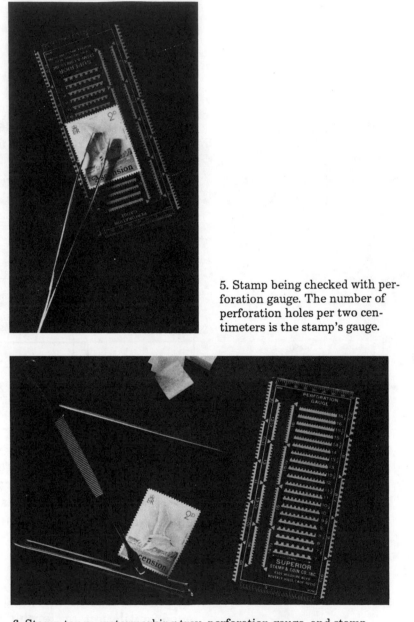

5. Stamp being checked with perforation gauge. The number of perforation holes per two centimeters is the stamp's gauge.

6. Stamp tongs, watermarking tray, perforation gauge, and stamp hinges — all necessary tools of the stamp collector.

CATALOGS   Every stamp collector needs a catalog. Even if you just have an inexpensive collection of worldwide pictorials, you'll learn more and be able to identify them better if you can compare your stamps with catalog pictures and descriptions. And no album that I know of has prices printed next to the stamp illustrations, so how can you estimate what your stamps are worth unless you have a catalog or price list?

Scott Catalogs   Scott Publishing Company, 911 Vandemark Road, Sidney, Ohio 45365 is the recognized source of standard stamp catalogs in the United States. Almost all dealer price lists for wholesale buying or retail selling, as well as virtually all U.S.-based auction companies, use Scott catalog numbers when listing a stamp.

Scott publishes five volumes every year, starting in the late spring with *Volume 1* (British Empire) and ending about November with the U.S. Specialized volume. Both soft and more expensive hardcover editions are available, and you don't necessarily need the latest edition if you collect stamps that don't change much in price. Your public library should have a set of Scott catalogs for reference and/or checking out.

Scott's *Volume 1* covers basic U.S. varieties, and then a fairly in-depth listing of Canada, Great Britain, and present and former British colonies. If you collect only British Empire stamps, this is the only Scott catalog you will need.

Volume 2 lists the stamps of countries beginning with the letters A through F. *Volume 3* has G-O countries, and *Volume 4* has the remainder of the alphabet, P-Z. Of course, *Volumes 2, 3* and *4* don't cover British Empire stamps which have their own listing in *Volume 1*.

Then there is the fifth volume, not numbered, but called the *Specialized Catalog of United States Stamps*, listing issues in great detail for all U.S. postal emissions, including regular postage, commemoratives, air mails, plate number blocks, first day covers, postal stationery (stamped envelopes and government postal cards), revenues, proofs, locals, souvenir cards, encased postage, Christmas seals, etc.

Of great importance are the listed varieties of nineteenth century U.S. stamps, many with prices indicated. For example, Scott U.S. #73, the two cent "Black Jack" stamp of 1863 is listed in three shades (black, gray-black, intense black); on regular cover, patriotic cover, and prisoner of war cover; as pairs, blocks, and plate number blocks; as a bisect on cover; printing varieties such as laid paper, printed on both sides, double transfers, short transfer, cracked plate; and twenty-three different cancels such as colored cancellations, "Ship Letter," and year dates.

Every serious dealer, collector, or investor of U.S. stamps needs a copy of Scott's *Specialized* catalog.

PRICE LISTS   You will also need recent price lists or auction catalog prices-realized tabulations to supplement and "make real" the theoretical values printed in the yearly catalogs. In the weekly stamp periodicals (discussed in Chapter 12) you will find many price lists with stated buy and sell prices for specific stamps. And many more of the dealers who take out small ads in the weeklies will be quite pleased to mail their next price list to you if you write to them and explain what you collect.

OTHER EQUIPMENT   Tongs, hinges, mounts, stock books, perforation gauge, watermark fluid, and a catalog are sufficient for most collectors to pursue a stamp hobby. But there are special items that some philatelists need: ultraviolet lamps for detecting repairs and post office "tagging," humidifying stamp boxes to facilitate separation in stamps that are stuck together, color charts, stamp drying books for use after soaking stamps off of envelopes, corner mounts for covers, and foreign catalogs.

Foreign Catalogs   Popular foreign catalogs available from some dealers are Gibbons (Britain), Michel (West Germany), Yvert (France), and Facit (Scandinavian countries). Standard stamp catalogs run $20 or more retail, and prices are always being adjusted to allow for profits, exchange rates, and increasing size of catalogs due to more stamp emissions.

Chapter 3

Stamp Manufacture

By knowing how a particular stamp is made, you can:

1. Better identify counterfeits produced by a different printing method or use of different inks or paper than the original.

2. See the difference between minor and major varieties because some production methods are more prone than others to create certain stamp varieties.

3. Learn the reasons why stamps look the way they do.

4. Distinguish different printing runs which are based on different papers, watermarks, inks, etc.

5. Better appreciate the artistic and technical subtleties that flourish on the stamps in your album.

PAPER Paper is made by grinding, heating, mixing, and bleaching various plant fibers so that they are changed into a *pulp*. This pulp is then poured onto a screen where the water drips off. The fibers used for stamps can come from wood, grass, cotton, and linen.

Better quality nineteenth century U.S. and foreign stamps had high levels of linen or cotton rags to make the paper tougher. Twentieth century issues are most often printed on cheap wood pulp papers, often with poor preserving characteristics. Many stamps that pre-date the Civil War are better preserved than stamps made after World War II.

Before the pulp is completely dry on the frame, it is compressed under pressure or rolled flat between rollers. If all goes well, the finished sheets of paper are smooth, evenly colored, and uniform in thickness. Coloring agents, binding chemicals, and silk threads may be added to the pulp at some stage of manufacture.

The two major types of paper used for stamps are wove and laid. Wove paper is a fine mesh, without light and dark lines when viewed against the light. Wove papers are smoother than laid papers. Laid paper is produced when the pulp is poured on parallel wires so that the final paper looks like alternating bars of light and dark areas, which in fact are due to the laid paper being thicker and thinner on adjacent lines.

Paper may be ordered in rolls or flat sheets by postal authorities. Slightly different shades, textures, or thicknesses in different batches of paper can result in interesting (and valuable?) varieties of the same stamp design. Collectors of British Empire issues tend to enjoy looking for paper varieties, and will sometimes pay high prices for specimens which their collections lack.

WATERMARKS

Watermarks are special designs impressed on paper during its manufacture, usually when the sheet is being pressed or rolled from the semi-dried pulp. The watermarked area is thinner than the surrounding paper, so it shows up as a darker part of the stamp's paper. Watermarks may be designed like letters of the alphabet, crowns, flowers, etc.:

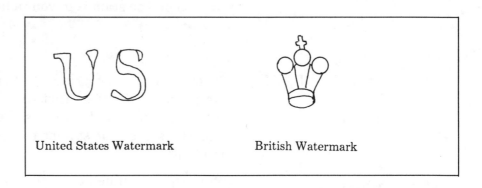

United States Watermark   British Watermark

Sometimes just a portion of a watermark will appear on any given stamp, and the poor impression of the watermark or an extraordinarily heavily cancelled stamp may obscure the watermark from easy identification. The standard catalogs show pictures and say which stamps are watermarked, so you can expect to find such marks in the paper of the stamps (see Chapter 2 to learn how to detect watermarks in stamps).

Watermark errors are avidly sought by collectors of British Commonwealth stamps. Inverted and sideways watermarks, the wrong design of watermark mistakenly used for a stamp, and the presence or absence of the mark when the opposite should be the case — all these are watermark errors which could greatly increase the market price of an otherwise common and cheap stamp! It pays to know which stamps have established watermark rarities so you can be on the lookout for them when browsing through a group of the normal versions.

STAMP DESIGN Before stamps can be manufactured, they must first be designed after being approved by postal officials. In the United States there is an organization within the reach of citizens who wish to propose a topic for a new stamp:

> Citizens' Stamp Advisory Committee
> c/o Stamp Development Branch
> U.S. Postal Service
> Washington, DC 20260

You can write to them and suggest a famous (or not so famous!) person, animal, historical event, sport, etc. for their consideration as a possible design for a new U.S. stamp. Better than individual letters would be to form a group for promoting a stamp design and officially submit serious, detailed proposals to the Committee.

The Committee consists of twelve to sixteen prominent citizens of varied backgrounds: education, art, history, business, etc., who are appointed for the sole purpose of debating the merits of proposed stamp designs, and sending their recommendations to the Postmaster General. The responsibility for selecting new stamp designs is his alone. Many Committee recommendations are accepted, but the final decision is always the Postmaster General's.

Once the subject is approved for a new stamp, the design is farmed out to various artists and production specialists whose job is to get the stamp designed, the printing methods outlined, and press run schedules prepared. Preliminary sketches need to be approved, and the final design worked up with colors appropriate to particular stamp presses at the Bureau of Engraving and Printing in Washington, DC.

There are four main methods of printing stamps: engraving, typography, photogravure, and lithography. Each of these methods requires quite different plate preparation techniques, so let's look at them individually.

Engraving Also known as *intaglio, recessed, incised*, and *line engraving*, the engraving process produces stamps of the most exquisite beauty with their delicate and razor sharp lines. American paper money is engraved. Take out a dollar bill and look at the fine lines in Washington's face, the scroll work around the border, the intricate details on the backside of the note.

Before the mid-1960s, virtually all United States stamps were engraved as an anti-counterfeiting measure and as a long-standing custom. Who would use a stamp from the post office if it wasn't engraved? If it had a "flat design"? If it looked like a Christmas seal or package label?

The first step in getting ready to engrave a stamp is to prepare a *master die*. This is a small piece of flat soft steel on which a Bureau engraver etches the stamp's design line by line, using a pointed steel tool harder than the master die. This tool is called a burin. Master die designs are indented into the die's surface.

After the design is completed on the master die, the die is hardened, and a roll of soft steel called the *transfer roll* is rocked into the master die. It picks up the die's design into a raised area on the transfer roll (known as the "relief"). The transfer roll is then hardened and its relief design is subsequently rolled into a soft steel *plate*.

This plate will print the stamps. The plate may be flat (*flat plate* printing) or curved (*rotary press*), and with modern machinery properly adjusted, the plate can print thousands upon thousands of sheets of stamps without showing signs of wear.

So we have master die, transfer roll, plate, and finished stamps when we are engraving. Great Britain's Penny Black, the first regular postage stamp in the world, was engraved in 1840. Likewise, the nineteenth century United States stamps were engraved.

Some minor errors (or printing varieties, depending on how you classify them!) found on engraved stamps are due to poorly transferred designs or touch-up work done after the master die was made. Reentries, double transfers, short transfers, and re-engraved stamps are common varieties among nineteenth century U.S. issues, especially those that pre-date the 1880s. As a rule, engraving varieties are worth slightly more than the normal version of the stamp.

One way that you can tell if a stamp is engraved is to lightly run your finger over its surface and feel the raised lines of ink on the paper. This is because the ink is forced into the recessed lines of the printing plate, and is therefore raised a little in relief on the paper when it dries. Engraving is very difficult to counterfeit. Sometimes a forgery is made of an engraved stamp by another printing method.

Typography   Typography is the opposite of engraving. In engraving, the stamp's design is cut below the surface of the plate which is inked and wiped clean for each printing impression. In typography, the design is raised above the plate's surface, and only the raised areas are inked for the printing:

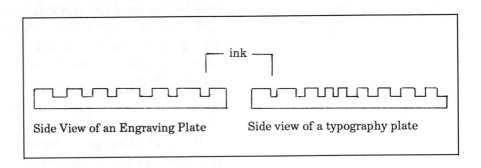

Side View of an Engraving Plate   Side view of a typography plate

If you've ever had printing shop as a class for junior or senior high school, you've worked with simple typography. The raised backwards letters on the little "quads" of type are the essence of typographic printing. The individual quadrats are pieces of hard metal with the raised typeface on the ends:

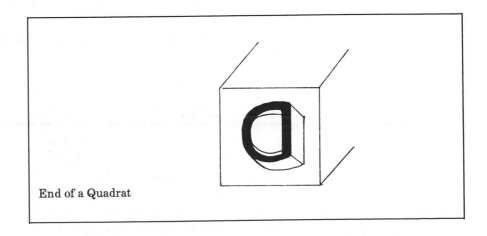

End of a Quadrat

Typography is also known as *letterpress* or *surface printing*. It can be distinguished from engraving by the lack of raised ink on the stamp's surface. On the other hand, typography, because it impresses the design into the stamp's paper, can often be identified by the raised areas which it gently pushes out on the back of the stamp. Engraved stamps are raised on their fronts, typographed stamps on their reverse sides.

The first U.S. stamp that was typographed was the 1846 City Despatch Post Carrier issue where the two cent surcharge was typographed over the original engraved stamp (Scott #6LB7). Many overprints are examples of typographic printing, because they are easy to prepare by setting up a group of similar quadrats or duplicating electrotypes of the original design.

One of my favorite typographed stamps is the U.S. commemorative honoring the Red Cross (Scott #1016), issued in 1952. The globe of the Earth and the rest of the stamp are engraved by rotary press, while the strikingly positioned cross is neatly typographed in with red ink.

Remember that the stamp's gum is applied in most cases after the ink impression on the front is printed, so if the gum is thick or if the printing pressure is light, it can be difficult to identify the stamp as being typographed if observed in mint condition. It could be lithographed.

Photogravure

Photogravure, also called *rotogravure* or *heliogravure* or in slang just *gravure*, is a printing method whereby the stamp's design is photographed through a fine screen which breaks up the image into many little dots. These dots are then etched onto a printing plate by chemical action. The dots are depressed below the plate's surface in a form similar to an engraved plate, but the relief effect on the printed stamp is too small to be felt as it can be with engraving.

The first U.S. stamp to be made by photogravure was the five cent commemorative honoring the artist Thomas Eakins (Scott #1335, issued in 1967). Many recent U.S. stamps have been printed all or in part by photogravure, and in my opinion they don't look nearly as handsome as U.S. engraved issues. Great Britain produces better stamps in photogravure than we do, and until we can do it as well, we should stick to what we do best — the quality line-engraved postage stamps once the standard of the world's stamp-issuing nations.

Under a magnifying glass a photogravured stamp should appear as fine dots of the same size and evenly spaced in the colored part of the stamp's design. And beware about soaking cancelled, photogravured stamps off of their envelopes: the ink may smear or totally dissolve in water (fugitive ink). You can remove such stamps from their paper backing by slightly moistening the back envelope paper until it pulls free of the stamp, being extremely careful not to get water on the stamp's front. Experiment with a few cheap photogravured stamps before trying it on an expensive example!

Lithography

Lithography is based on the principle that oil and water don't mix. The stamp's design is drawn on a printing plate with a greasy material that attracts the ink. The plate is wet with water or an acid mixture that fills the areas of the plate where no design exists, and rejects the printing ink in those places, causing the ink to concentrate on the oily designed portion. Then the stamp sheet is printed by pressing it against the plate.

Under magnification, photolithography (a combination of photographic transfer processes and lithography) makes stamps appear to be designed with little dots like in photogravure, *but* in lithography the dots aren't uniform in size or distribution. Very smooth paper is also used for most lithographed stamps. Lithographed lines are not raised on the stamp's front (engraved) or depressed on the stamp's back (typographed).

Lithography is also known as *offset* printing. It is the cheapest process for printing stamps, but lithographed stamps may still be expensive in the stamp market due to supply and demand. Ugly appearances and inexpensive production may never sell furniture or clothes, but stamp collectors are attracted to various stamps for many reasons, not merely aesthetic ones.

Besides some revenues and Post Office seals, the first use of lithography for U.S. stamps was the regular issues of 1918-1920 (Scott #525-536). There were material and labor shortages in World War I, so these issues weren't engraved as usually was done with U.S. stamps.

INK

The inks employed in postage stamp manufacture are derived from natural minerals and are mixed to get a uniform consistency and color standard. Heavy inking of the printing plate, heavy pressure during printing the stamp sheet, and darker pigments in the ink mixture will produce darker stamps.

While most ink used for stamps is more or less waterproof, care must be taken when soaking or otherwise moistening (such as hinging a stamp from the front side to display the gum) certain stamps because they are printed with fugitive inks. Photo gravured stamps, aniline-based dyes, and some safety papers will tend to dissolve in the presence of water, so be careful when working with them. Fugitive-inked stamps are best kept away from the watermark tray also; try discerning their watermarks by holding them up to the light or using one of the special electronic watermark detectors for sale by stamp dealers.

Ink fades with time. Strong light, especially sunlight, will change the brilliance of a fresh stamp to a dull color by the bleaching effect of the light's rays. Don't pay a lot of money for a stamp color error unless it is accompanied by an expertizing certificate (see Chapter 9). Stamp ink colors can be readily altered by chemical processes which bleach, add, or remove one or more colors.

SHADES

The collection of true shades is a popular specialty among certain philatelists. For example, the three cent Victory issue of 1919 (Scott U.S. #537) is listed in the Scott catalog for $11 mint in the common violet shade, but in deep red-violet it is priced at $325 mint (Scott #537a). And to complicate matters, the catalog cites two more shades: light reddish violet (Scott #537b, $11 mint) and red violet (Scott #537c, $40 mint)!

So how can you tell which Victory shade it is? By comparing a questionable stamp's color against a known stamp's shade, by buying from a reliable dealer who has color vision as precise as his honest business ethics, and by insisting on getting an expertizing certificate guaranteeing the shade when buying expensive color varieties.

The U.S. Civil War three cent regular issue of 1861 (Scott #65) is listed in Scott's catalog at $50 mint in the most common shade, rose. But if it can be found in pink, it becomes the rare and desirable #64, cataloging $3,500 mint and $250 just for used ones! Every U.S. classics stamp dealer, as well as expertizing services, gets inquiries about #65's whose owners are firmly convinced that they possess the more valuable #64.

The true #64 has a slight bluish cast to the primary pink shade, and the pink color is markedly different from the common rose variety (#65). But all these three cent varieties have notoriously discolored over the past hundred-plus years, and further manipulating by an unscrupulous stamp "doctor" could lighten the color of a common rose stamp and pass it off as the expensive pink variety.

GUM   Gum is the glue that is applied to the back of a stamp's sheet for the future purpose of being moistened so the stamp sticks to an envelope.

The first gum used on stamps was the potato, wheat, and acacia formula which was spread on the backs of the Penny Blacks of Great Britain in 1840. In the last third of the nineteenth century, a dextrine gum became widespread for stamp production, and in the late 1960s the polyvinyl alcohol gums were introduced to inhibit mint stamp curling.

Some stamps were issued without gum, some with more than one gum type, and some with the wrong gum than the type originally authorized. Many stamps of China have been issued without gum; a container of glue was placed in post offices for affixing Chinese stamps on mail.

Self-sticking gums have been used on a limited basis for U.S. stamps (like Scott #1552, the ten cent Peace Dove issue) and certain foreign stamps (like Tonga self-adhesive issues, for example Scott #C58-C82). Collectors generally don't like these stamps because the self-adhering gum stains albums when it ages, is hard to remove, and basically isn't traditional in a hobby like philately where tradition exerts strong pressure.

Remember that gum is put on stamps *before* they are perforated, so the gum shouldn't drip over onto the front of the stamp unless it has been disturbed (including fraudulently reapplied) since it left the post office.

PERFORATIONS   Perforations are the little holes that are punched out between adjacent stamp designs to facilitate stamp separation for postal use. The first stamps to be governmentally perforated were Great Britain's issues in 1853-1855 (Scott #8-9), including the early experimental trials. In 1855 Swedish perforated stamps appeared, followed by Norway in 1856, the U.S. in 1857, and Canada in 1858. By the late 1860s, perforations had essentially replaced the former imperforate (unperforated) stamp format whereby stamps had to be cut from their sheets with scissors.

Perforation varieties include fine, coarse, rough, blind (not punched all the way through), compound (two different gauges on the same stamp), double rows, misperforated (holes cut the stamp's design), and the absence or presence of perforations when the opposite was the way they were commonly issued. Imperforate stamps (lacking all perforations, and having at least an adjacent pair to verify it) from normally perforated varieties are the most expensive perforation errors in rare stamps, typically several hundred dollars or more per pair. But believe it or not, some U.S. coil rolls have been discovered imperforated in such quantities that they sell for $10 or less per imperforate pair!

Nowadays we have "electric eye" machines that line up the perforations neatly between the stamp designs, resulting in excellent perforation alignment on most U.S. stamps issued after World War II. So accurate are these that most U.S. commemoratives of the last forty years are rare in misperforated form (until most recently when quality seems to have been slipping). The electric eye device was first used on perforating machinery for U.S. stamps in 1933 for distribution to local post offices in 1935 (Scott #634 printing variety).

OTHER PRINTING ADDITIONS

Besides the paper, ink, gum, and perforations which make our stamps, there a few other things that may be present in the finished product. "Tagging" has been a recent addition to stamp routine production in which the stamps are coated with luminescent material (*fluorescent* or *phosphorescent*, glowing under ultraviolet light, and still glowing after the light is turned off, respectively) which is recognized by automatic sorting equipment. The standard catalogs tell which stamps have been so "tagged," and by buying an ultraviolet lamp for $20 to $40 you can observe and classify such issues in your home.

Overprints, including surcharges and precancels, are usually typographed onto a finished stamp for rate changes, town identification, war provisional use, etc. Inverted overprints, sideways varieties, double overprints, different colors than the normal, and partially or completely lacking overprints are highly coveted by specialists, and are often cataloged at steep prices.

Various printing errors include paper inclusions (dust or other tiny materials visible in the finished stamp), printed on both sides, partial prints, dry plates (underinked engravings), wrong colors on multicolored stamps, double impressions (similar to the "doubled die" familiar to coin collectors: the 1955 Lincoln cent error), albinos (no ink used at all, usually referring to embossed postal stationery), special printings on different paper, wrong perforation size, pre-printing paper folds and creases, inverted centers on multicolored hand-fed sheets, ghost plate numbers in the selvage outside the stamps on the panes, overinking, plate smears, wrong paper used, etc.

It is important to realize that just because it is an error doesn't make it valuable. *Supply* and *demand* when working together are the only factors that make things valuable in a free market. And the stamp market most often is, when informed collectors and dealers do business.

Chapter 4

Condition

Condition determines the price of a stamp as much as anything else. The rarest thing in the world looks ugly if it is broken down, damaged beyond recognition, and appears to have been retrieved from a junk yard. Only the stamps of the highest scarcity and in the highest demand will command a decent price in damaged condition. Think of what they might bring if they were in excellent shape!

There are certain unique (one-of-a-kind!) high demand stamps that are valuable due to their romantic history and strong philatelic interest. An example is the most expensive stamp in existence, the one cent British Guiana of 1856. Its four corners are cut off, but it sold in 1980 for close to $1,000,000. The Hawaiian missionaries (Scott Hawaii #1-4) are listed in the Scott catalog at between $9000 and $250,000 each in off cover state, and virtually all known copies are damaged.

But for lesser philatelic items that average mortals buy, condition greatly influences the price paid and the ultimate resale value if the stamps are held a while for investment.

CENTERING The relationship between the design and the unprinted space between the design and the edge of the stamp's paper is what makes up the quality called *centering*. A well-centered stamp is more pleasing to look at than a badly off-center one, and collectors will readily pay more for a nicely centered stamp that normally is found off-center.

In order, from best to worst, the centering grades in philately most generally accepted are Superb, Extremely Fine, Very Fine, Fine, and Very Good.

Superb A *superb* (S or SUP) stamp is flawless to the naked eye. It has rich color, full perforations or wide margins if an imperforate variety, full undamaged gum if mint, lightly cancelled if used, as perfectly centered as visually feasible, and with absolutely no defects like surface scrapes, thins, or tears.

Stamps made after World War II are often found in what is essentially superb condition, but most of them are so common and cheap to buy that the pretentiousness of calling them "superb" is a bit meaningless. Superb as a stamp grade is best reserved for describing older stamps that miraculously have been found in a wonderful state of preservation, especially if they are notorious for being normally found heavily off center.

It is pretty hard to make a perfect drawing, but I'll give it a try with a sketch of an imperforate stamp and its perforated cousin, both of which I hope look like they are perfectly centered:

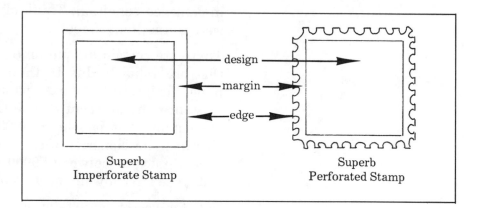

Conservative graders rarely use the term superb. Some stamp dealers use it all the time in their price lists and auction catalogs. Let's just say that if a stamp is truly superb, it cannot be improved upon, and everybody who sees it will agree that it is superb. If informed philatelists have their doubts about a superb stamp's alleged grade, then maybe it belongs in the next category.

Extremely Fine   For practical collecting and buying/selling purposes, about the best we can expect in nineteenth century U.S. stamps is the grade of *extremely fine* (EF or XF). An extremely fine stamp is ever so slightly off-center, but closely approaching superb centering. Of course, it has no damages, but has original gum (that may be a bit disturbed or lightly hinged) if mint. If cancelled, the cancel ink is light and does not detract from the stamp's overall beauty.

Notice how these extremely fine stamps are only a little off-center, and are nicely cancelled in one corner away from the major part of the stamp's design:

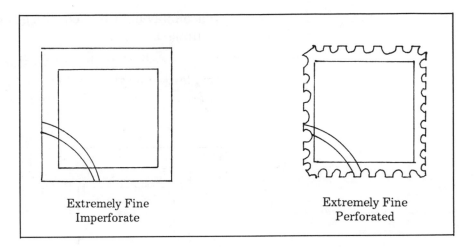

Extremely Fine
Imperforate

Extremely Fine
Perforated

When liberal graders talk about superb stamps (especially if they are selling them!), they usually mean extremely fine quality. They have an honest or dishonest opinion that their stamps are perfect, even though they are visibly off-center to a small degree.

Some auction catalogs avoid the words *superb* and *extremely fine* almost entirely, while others sprinkle them into many of their stamp descriptions. The point is, look at the stamp and decide for yourself if it is indeed approaching perfection, or perhaps deserves a grade of *very fine*.

Very Fine   There's nothing horribly wrong with a *very fine* (VF) stamp; it is not perfect, that's all! Most of the stamps in a high quality collection will probably grade *very fine*. Such stamps have a ready market for buying or selling, and will satisfy all but the most discriminating collectors who insist on near impeccability, known as "condition cranks" by dealers who can't find stamps that fit such collectors' high standards.

Sometimes you'll see a stamp offered for sale with this description: "*Very fine* centering, tiny thin, small tropical paper stain in the margin, surface scuff." In my opinion, that stamp is damaged and should never be insulted with a label of "very fine" when in reality it is such only in centering. It is like advertising a car in "great condition" except that it is missing a few wheels and part of the motor.

Very fine stamps may be quite off center when matched next to a properly graded extremely fine example. But the design is well clear of the edge or perforations, and the cancellation is reasonably light if used, the gum is partly or completely present if unused.

Can you see that these two stamps are off-center but still have two large margins, and the other two margins are fairly clear of the stamp's edge? They are *very fine*:

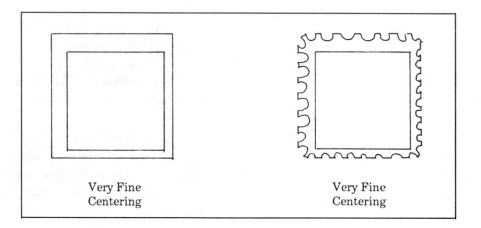

Very Fine
Centering

Very Fine
Centering

The best very fine stamps, in my opinion, are those which are balanced with opposite margins of equal width. The stamp is still off-center, but it is equally off-center:

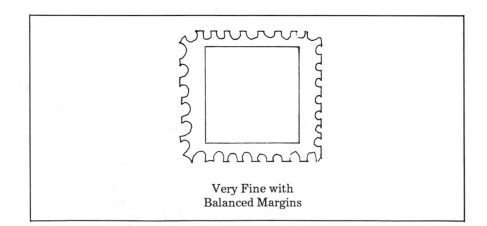

Very Fine with
Balanced Margins

The above stamp might be called *superb* or "extremely fine with boardwalk margins on three sides" if the grader is liberal. To me, it is a nice stamp but because it is off-center, I prefer, by conservatively calling it *very fine*, to establish a sincere standard of perfection whereby superb and extremely fine grades are worth something.

You can call anything whatever you want, but that doesn't make it so! If you think that you have an extremely fine or superb stamp, take it to a dealer and try to sell it, and see what he says about the grade. If an informed buyer honestly thinks a stamp is very fine, then it could well be very fine for all we know; or it could be merely *fine*.

Fine   The word "fine" has a higher value when used to describe your health when someone asks, "How are you?" than it has when put as a label on a stamp's grade. *Fine* (F) stamps are not damaged unless stated otherwise, have their designs clear of the perforations although it may be close, and if cancelled are not totally obliterated, if unused have some of the original gum unless otherwise noted.

Fine stamps are acceptable to the majority of collectors, but for investment or condition-oriented, award-winning exhibits you would try to get very fine items. A sound (undamaged) fine stamp has nothing intrinsically wrong with it. The centering is just significantly off:

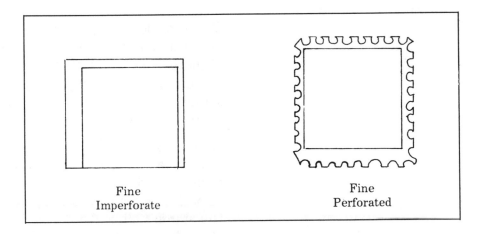

Fine
Imperforate

Fine
Perforated

Often you'll find price lists or auction catalogs describing nineteenth century stamps as "fine for the year of issue," indicating that those stamps should be tolerated in worse condition because they are commonly encountered with damaged perforations, awful centering, etc. That's the same as declaring: "We've got a healthy horse here, except that it has a broken leg and poor eyesight because it is twenty years old."

Either a stamp is fine or it isn't. What does "for year of issue" mean anyway? Fine stamps are those whose designs are clear of the perforations (or paper's edge in the case of imperforates). If the design is cut into the stamp's edge, it is not fine, it is at the most *very good*.

Very Good   *Very good* (VG) stamps are heavily off-center with the design cut by the stamp's edge:

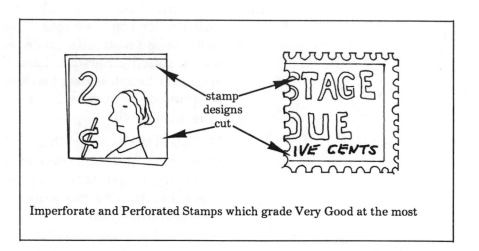

Imperforate and Perforated Stamps which grade Very Good at the most

Some dealers will also grade a stamp very good if the perforations are chewed up, if there is a small tear or thin, and if there is a crease that doesn't cut all the way through the stamp's paper. Strictly "very good" means that the stamp is sound (undamaged) but that the design is just cut into by the perforations or the stamp's edge for imperforates.

Early U.S. issues, like Scott #1 and #2 (the first two regularly issued, general use U.S. stamps) are described as having four or three margins, etc., referring to how many sides of the imperforate stamp are completely clear between the design and the stamp's edge. A four-margined imperforate, no matter how close the margins, technically grades *fine* if it is not damaged. A three-margined stamp (also called "cut into one side") grades *very good* by conservative rules. The selling price of four-margined imperforate early U.S. or foreign stamps is significantly greater than those whose designs are cut.

Should you ever buy a very good stamp? Yes, if you can't afford a fine copy and don't care to recover much of your purchase price. Or if it is an extreme rarity, only obtainable with such poor centering. Or if the price is so ridiculously low, even for such inferior material, that it seems appealing for its own sake (for example, a $5 Columbian commemorative, Scott U.S. #245, cataloging $3600 unused, offered for sale in sound, very good condition for fifty dollars).

The Lowest Grades   Depending on whom you talk to, stamps can be further graded below *very good* in this descending order: *good, fair,* and *poor.* What constitutes the distinction between these inferior grades is debatable, but let's say that they are damaged stamps with one of these devastating defects: a completely obliterating cancel that hides virtually the whole stamp design, a large tear through a major portion of the stamp, one or more pin holes observable with the naked eye, major pieces of the stamp's paper torn off, serious ink scrapes on the surface, creases that have ruined the stamp's paper integrity, large thins, large stains, severe color changes due to weathering, fading, chemical processes after issue, or no appreciable margins.

Only great rarities should be bought in grades below very good, and then only with expert advice from trusted philatelists and experienced dealers. If you can afford to buy the stamp in sound condition, and can locate one for sale, why buy it damaged? A damaged stamp is always defective and constantly carries with it the stigma of undesirability. For investment or serious exhibition competition, sound material is deeply impressive and most profitable in the long run.

Split Grades   Since grading is subjective, and because some stamps may display characteristics of two adjacent grades, you will often see a stamp listed as grading Fine to Very Fine (F-VF), or slightly better than Very Fine (VF+). These are not necessarily fraudulent business tactics by loose graders who are trying to separate you from your money, although sometimes they are! They most often mean that in the seller's honest opinion, the stamp grades between two standard grades and is so designated in both the split grade and in its price which should fall in between the normal prices for each of those grades. For example, an F-VF stamp might sell for $15, if F is priced at $10, and VF at $25.

Average   *Average* (AV or AVG) is the same as very good to fine (VG-F) for many philatelists. Average means not of high quality, and a dealer who advertises average stamps for sale is telling you not to expect much. Average could also be used to describe damaged stamps. At any rate, expect the worst when you are buying average quality, and if you receive anything better than design-cut, off center, damaged items, consider yourself lucky!

And then you'll notice ads which state, "Average, for the year of issue," or "Average very fine." What can you make of this generalized stuff? If a stamp is average very fine, what would unaverage very fine look like? And if the year of issue is normally encountered off-center, very good to fine (VG-F), then why not state that grade and reduce some of the mystery in such a transaction?

COLOR   A stamp's color influences its condition evaluation. Light has a tendency to fade a stamp's color, so you should never display rare stamps constantly in the rays of strong light, especially sunlight or strong fluorescent light. While the superb through poor grading scale explained in the first part of this chapter is mostly used to describe a stamp's centering, it is an unwritten rule in the stamp market that other factors are implicitly understood when calling a stamp by a standard grade classification. For example, a superb stamp that is badly faded can hardly still be known as superb. And the only way to verify a stamp's true color is to compare it with genuine stamps of the same type. An experienced collector or dealer can often pass judgment on a stamp's color as a result of years of handling similar stamps.

Bright color, as close to the original shade as can possibly be determined, is desired in rare stamps and will raise their price over dull-colored specimens.

GUM   Gum is the most valuable thing on Earth, according to Herman Herst, Jr., the famous New York stamp dealer who is now retired. By weight, gum is more expensive than diamonds, gold, or uranium. Gum is the glue that postal agencies place on the backs of stamps during their manufacture, and gum fanatics will pay astronomical prices to get original undisturbed gum on a rare stamp.

Let's summarize by saying that stamps that have damaged gum are much harder to sell than never hinged (NH) original gum (OG) specimens. Knowledgeable dealers and collectors appreciate lightly hinged stamps, but many modern investors and newer dealers think that a light hinge mark completely destroys a stamp's value.

And it very much depends on whether you are buying or selling. Dealers with loose ethics and questionable moral standards will not mention the disturbed gum on a stamp they are trying to sell to you, but will scream about how awful it looks when you go to sell it back to them. The fact is that rare and popular stamps are saleable in unused, full gum, lightly hinged condition, and that price is more often obtained at auction than in a dealer's shop.

Collectors in Europe will often pay double or triple the price of a stamp if it is never hinged perfect gum, as opposed to a lightly hinged copy. Not necessarily intelligent, but a market fact that we must forever keep in mind when buying or selling mint stamps.

To preserve your investment, never hinge a mint, unhinged rare stamp. Store it on an approval card in a stock book, or mount it with hingeless plastic mounts on an album page.

If all the gum is washed off of a stamp, but it has never been cancelled, it is called *unused*. Strict graders reserve *mint* for never hinged stamps. Unused stamps can typically be bought for half the cost of a nice full-gummed version.

Regumming

Since the craze for collecting never hinged (NH) stamps began in the 1920s, and has accelerated in the intervening years, many regum artists have sprung up to make money from collectors obsessed with getting what they think is pristine gum. All gum ages, and nineteenth century gum is usually discolored (often yellowed), cracked, and more or less dried out. But if an unused stamp has no gum, it is tempting for a crook to buy it, regum it, and pass it off as an original gum specimen at a hefty profit.

The U.S. Postal Inspection Service advises that mail order fraud is partly the customer's fault: "If it looks too good to be true, it probably is!" This applies especially to evaluating the gum on an old stamp. Gum should look its age. Hundred year old gum shouldn't have the smoothness and snap of the gum on the stamps bought last week at your post office.

Some tips for detecting faked gum on regummed stamps:

1. It looks too good for its age.

2. It doesn't match the gum appearance of similar stamps of the time period.

3. It seems to have dribbled over onto the *front* of the stamp

(basically impossible on original gummed stamps).

4. It seems abnormally thick or thin in places.

5. The "teeth" between the stamp's perforation holes are a bit stiff and brittle due to the regumming operation. The fake gum has soaked into the torn paper fibers around the perforation holes.

6. The texture, color, or feel of the gum just doesn't look right when compared with normal mint stamps of the time period.

7. The selling price seems too low, an indication of possible fraudulent merchandise in any business.

8. The particular stamps in question are virtually unknown in undisturbed original gum mint state. You expect modern stamps to have nice gum. You don't expect to see somebody walk in the room and drop a dozen copies of U.S. #1 or Great Britain #1 (the five cent Franklin and the Penny Black, the first two regular issues of the U.S. and Britain) on the table, each one with flawless, pristine unhinged gum.

Some expertizing services will comment on the gum when they issue an expertizing certificate (see Chapter 9), stating that it is or is not original gum, in their professional opinion. Because gum changes the price so much for rare mint stamps, get an expertizing certificate when you are buying an expensive mint stamp if you doubt your own judgment on the gum's authenticity.

OTHER PRICE DEPRESSANTS

Any of these detracting factors can lower a stamp's perceived condition and therefore its price: reperforation, faked perforations, faked cancels, faked color, paper added to fill out a thin, fraudulently added watermarks, drawn-in parts of the design to replace scuffed areas, added guide lines on coil pairs, altered plate numbers, rejoined blocks, etc. If any of these are present, their grade changes to a special category called "Repaired." It is okay to buy or sell damaged and repaired stamps, provided that the buyer and seller know exactly what is being offered. It is against the law to misrepresent stamps, not to sell the damaged ones by advertising them for what they really are!

Chapter 5

Specializing

Most people start in stamp collecting by saving stamps of the whole world. When I was seven years old, my uncle gave me a cheap paperback stamp album, a small packet of general foreign stamps, and hinges for mounting them in the album. I would spend time after school with my Dad, trying to find where each stamp belonged in the album, identifying the countries and time periods. My Dad had a collection when he was a boy and he showed me how to use hinges and how to pick up a stamp safely if you drop it on the floor (moisten your finger tip with your tongue and then lightly touch the stamp with the damp finger — it usually adheres to your skin until you can bring the stamp back up to the table top).

From a school child's first album to an international stamp exhibition award-winning collection is a long way. A typical person gets introduced to philately as a pre-teenager, is distracted and busy with other affairs and concerns in high school and college or employment after high school. Then in his mid to late twenties remembers the fun and excitement with stamps as a kid, and decides to pull out the old collection and resume "stamping."

THE EXCITEMENT OF STAMPS

And fascinating it is to plunge into the world of stamps and what they represent: a paper documentary artifact of a special time in history of a nation's governmental postal functions. Who hasn't dreamed of exotic lands with wild animals and unexplored forests? You can see these things on the stamps of Africa.

Hitler and Stalin parade across the stamps of Germany and Russia. Coconut palms grace the issues from Pacific Islands, while railroad train commemoratives and jet planes in flight are pictured on the postal paper of industrial countries. Marching soldiers, circus clowns, pretty puppies, and sports players are all found on stamps.

Doesn't it excite you to receive an unexpected letter from some overseas post office? Who sent it? What does it say? Where were those strange stamps made and how long did it take to get here?

Many a famous philatelist began collecting by clipping stamps off of the incoming family mail. Holiday and birthday presents of stamp packets have often been responsible for turning on the stamp curiosity of a youthful mind. Geography lessons and history reports have been enhanced with stamp visual aids, eventually leading to a lifetime passion for acquiring and studying these little bits of paper, these emissaries of time.

THE REASONS FOR SPECIALIZATION

About 500,000 major types of stamps have been issued by the world's governments. Since nobody can ever hope to complete a collection of all of these issues, due to financial limits or the impossibility of tracking down elusive items, most collectors decide to specialize. There are many types of specialized collections, each tailor-made for the person's taste.

Time is another consideration when choosing a specialty. If you're young and healthy and expect to earn a reasonable middle class income over the next thirty-five years, you can embark on an ambitious program of collecting all U.S. issues or all of the world's special deliveries, for example. If you're eighty-five years old, in somewhat frail health, and living on social security, a more modest album of British postage dues or Japanese picture postcards might be wise.

Specialized collections tend to sell more readily than a hodgepodge. A solid run of Austrian semi-postals (charity stamps) from the first one issued in 1914 (Franz Josef monarchy stamps, Scott #B1-B2) to the present time would be easy to sell to a dealer or collector/investor of twentieth century Austria.

Knowledge limitation is another constraint in forcing a collector to specialize. No one can possibly know even the basics of all the stamps ever printed. Some philatelists spend their whole lives investigating a short series of regular issues or even a single stamp variety, and conclude their massive studies by saying that they haven't exhausted their subjects.

Just as it is easier to buy an encyclopedia than to read it, the enthusiastic stamp collector finds that it is a simple matter to purchase items, a very exhausting pursuit to learn about them. Knowledge is power, and the astute philatelist specializes in a certain country, time period, types of cancels, or a topical subject (like cats or maps on stamps) by reading what is known about the specialty, buying and selling stamps in that specialty, and profiting financially and intellectually as a result of the time invested.

It is common for a specialist to recognize the value of a rare item, enabling the clever purchase of it, possibly at a low price.

Finally, a specialized group of stamps and covers makes artistic and emotional sense. Would you rather have a couple of hundred different things with little relationship among them or an exquisite, exhibition quality set of U.S. definitives or French prisoner of war envelopes?

TYPES OF SPECIALTIES

Mint Stamps

Mint stamps are a logical specialty, regardless of what country you are collecting. Mint means post office fresh, as nice as the day it was first sold, allowing for minor effects of normal aging. A mint stamp has clean paper, good ink color, and full undisturbed original gum on the back. If it is undamaged it is usually worth the most money for the particular issue, being more expensive to buy than unused or used, but bringing a heftier price when it is eventually sold.

Mint stamps look nice because there are no obstructing cancels or postal markings, and their gum verifies their mint status — evidence that they are not merely used stamps that have had their cancels chemically removed.

Mint stamps are rare for some issues and therefore in high demand for investment, exhibition, and philatelic purposes. A mint portfolio of high-demand rarities is a blue chip collection, easy to sell or auction off. And cheap stamps should be bought in mint condition because they aren't much more expensive that way than they would be if they were unused or cancelled.

Unused Stamps

Unused stamps have never been cancelled but lack their original gum on the back. Unused stamps are typically available for fifty percent or less of the mint price for the issue. A collector of limited budget or one who wants to exhibit the front of the stamps may select unused rather than mint to stretch the hobby dollar.

Investors and dealers tend to shy away from unused stamps

because they are harder to sell than mint. And if the gum has questionable authenticity, the stamp is automatically labelled unused instead of mint, reducing its value and desirability.

Beware of unused stamps masquerading as mint by having faked gum added. If you can't identify original gum, buy from a money-back guarantee dealer or get an expensive mint stamp expertized so that you'll know it wasn't an unused stamp with doctored gum, manufactured to get your hard-earned cash.

Used Stamps   *Used stamps* have been cancelled. They are often obtainable for a fraction of the mint price. Wonderful cancellation collections have been built up consisting solely of used stamps.

For example, the U.S. commemorative set of Columbians, issued for the World's Columbian Exposition held in Chicago during the summer of 1893 to honor the 400th anniversary of the discovery of America (Scott #230-245), has a catalog value of $13,313.50 unused and $5,657.86 used. You can buy a used set of Columbians for less than half the price of a mint set, centering and other factors being equal.

Also, some stamps are known for their extensive and intricate array of cancels, making them ideal candidates for a specialized study or for an investment portfolio.

Many German issues from before World War II are worth more with genuine cancels than they are in mint condition, and it becomes a challenge to find them with genuine cancels dated properly from the time period when the stamps were current.

Another plus is that you don't have to be paranoid about the back of a stamp when you buy cancelled ones; there's no gum to protect or expertize.

Multiples   *Multiples* like blocks of four, plate number blocks, coil strips, used pairs, or strips used on cover are interesting specialties for the collector with a deeper purse. It is unnecessary for a representative collection to include multiples, but it enhances its value and interest.

Some spectacular accumulations of early U.S. mint blocks have been formed over the years, and they always produce spirited bidding and decent prices when put up for auction.

Full Panes   *Full panes* are what the average person calls "sheets" of stamps.

A pane is the largest sized format of a stamp that is sold over the counter in the post office.

Special albums and storage files made of acid-free paper and plastic interleaving are used to store panes of stamps. It is expensive, but occasionally profitable to buy stamps in full panes. A collection of rare or early panes is truly a marvel to behold, not to mention its high monetary value!

Covers

Covers are envelopes or cards, with or without adhesive stamps affixed, that were meant to be used as mail communication. First-day covers with stamps officially cancelled on the first day of issue are the most common covers collected by beginners. Rare classic covers of elusive nineteenth century stamps of the world and modern commercial (not prepared by stamp collectors) covers fall into the category of "postal history," a lively specialty at this time.

Examples of cover collections are first-day covers of a single type of stamp, covers cancelled in your own hometown, envelopes carried by private couriers outside of the official mails, post cards from a country or time period, war mail, censored mail, special use mail (like air mail covers, postage dues, etc.), local use covers, trans-oceanic mail, and expedition envelopes either commercially or philatelically inspired.

Errors, Freaks, and Oddities

Errors, freaks, and *oddities* are another stamp specialty. Off center stamps, missing perforation holes, color errors, doubly printed stamps, multiple perforations, printed on both sides, wrong paper, wrong watermarks, and inverted images are errors that have their admirers and customers. Errors are almost always worth more than the normal stamps, but not necessarily a "fortune" because supply and demand still play a part in determining the price.

Postal Stationery

Postal stationery is a subspecialty of cover collecting. Postal stationery is defined as items sold by post offices for immediate use as mail transmission paper. Examples are postal cards, embossed stamped envelopes, and foldable aerograms. Postal stationery is collected both in mint and cancelled forms. It tends to be less valuable than stamps of the same time period because fewer people collect stationery than collect postage stamps.

7. Two cent "Black Jack" regular issued during Civil War. Earliest known use July 6, 1863. Catalog value $20 used. Catalog #73.

8. Stampless Cover: Philadelphia to New York to London. A ship letter, left New York June 19, arrived in Liverpool on July 10 (backstamped). Transit time: New York to Liverpool in 21 days. Before the use of general U.S. stamps in this country (1847), all letters overseas were sent without adhesive stamps, better known as "stampless covers" in philately.

9. Engelbert Dollfuss ten schillings dark blue Austrian issue of July 25, 1936, issued for the second anniversary of the chancellor's death. Catalog value $675 mint, $900 used (more for used than mint!). Copies exist imperforated at $2500 catalog value. Catalog #Austria 380.

10. Baseball three cent commemorative First Day Cover cancelled June 12, 1939 at Cooperstown, New York. Catalog value $18 as a first day cover. Catalog #855.

Single Countries   *Single countries* are wise specialties. You can concentrate on the issues of one nation and assemble either a mint or used album of them. Whole books have been written on the stamps of certain countries, and these publications are easily purchased from philatelic literature dealers.

A "dead country" is a political entity that no longer exists, but once issued its own stamps. Estonia and Latvia are examples of once independent stamp-issuing governments that are now politically part of the Soviet Union. An advantage of collecting a dead country is that you know approximately how much it will cost you to complete your collection since all of its stamps are known.

An advantage of collecting a country that still exists is that you can obtain new issues every year to keep your interest in the collection, and the inhabitants of that country, if they have disposable income, tend to keep upward price pressure on their nation's stamps. A disadvantage of collecting a "live country" is that modern world events and collector fads can produce wild price swings either up or down for its stamps. Dead countries have more stable and constant prices.

Stamps of a country usually sell for the best prices within that country rather than somewhere else.

Limited Time Periods   *Limited time periods* make nice collections. You can acquire all of the stamps made in every country during your birth year. Or you could build a collection of post-World War I Egyptian definitives. Or western European issues of the 1950s. Or twentieth century U.S. commemoratives. Or air mail covers since the invention of the jet airplane.

Single Usage Stamps   *Single usage stamps* are great collecting goals. Some collectors just save the air mail issues of one country, global area, or of the whole world. Postage dues, semi-postals, overprinted revalued stamps, special deliveries, regular issues (definitives), commemoratives, revenues, officials, hunting and fishing documentaries, booklet panes, locals, specimens, essays, and proofs are stamps printed for specific purposes.

The specialized collection is the way most serious collectors and investors deal with stamps. It is possible to pick an interesting specialty, find and buy the appropriate stamps, study them, discover new facts about them, and become something of an expert on them. And you have a waiting market for your collection if your chosen specialty is also the specialty of other people.

Topical Collecting

Topical collecting is always fun and can be inexpensive. Topicals are stamps with one theme in their pictures: sports, birds, rocks, airplanes, famous women, trees, spaceships, etc. Topical collectors tend to try to get comprehensive collections of such specialized topics from the world's stamp issues. Catalog illustrations and a friendly dealer willing to supply topical issues are the starting points of such a collection.

Chapter 6

Buying Stamps

Free stamps are either hard to come by or don't fit in a serious collection because they aren't varied enough or are too cheap. You can get stamps for free by clipping cancelled copies off your incoming mail, asking friends and relatives to save stamps for you, or getting a local business, church, or other organization to save cancelled stamps for you. If you work in the mail room of a major company it may be possible to get permission to take home the cancelled stamps that the company receives on its mail. And then there are holidays and your birthday when you may request stamps as presents.

But how do you obtain the older issues? More expensive investment-class varieties? Covers postmarked before you were born? Errors and printing states? Stamps from obscure nations?

Buying stamps is necessary for the dedicated philately student or stamp investor. And it is important to remember that different methods of buying have their own advantages and disadvantages.

HOW TO SELECT A DEALER Dealers are human. You'll find every type of person if you make the rounds of America's professional stamp dealers. Some are young, some old, their knowledge and philatelic expertise having little to do with their age or number of years in the business!

Some dealers are friendly and extroverted; others shy and quiet. Some will explain in great detail the stamps in their stock and don't immediately care whether you buy or not. Others hardly give you the time of day unless you flash a roll of paper money and declare your intention to buy a lot from them.

Most stamp businesses are honestly run. A few are crooks and use borderline ethics to make a quick buck. Some dealers will accept your check or credit card. Some insist on cash or equivalent value stamps in trade.

In the telephone book Yellow Pages under the heading "Stamps for Collectors," you'll discover the names and business addresses of your local stamp shops. It is always a good idea to visit and patronize a local dealer: they're close to home, they get to know you and your needs, and they can be used as a source of ready cash if you have to sell some stamps for emergency funds.

Find a dealer who has the type of material that you want, whom you feel comfortable doing business with, and who has reasonable prices for both buying and selling.

PRECAUTIONS IN BUYING

There's a saying in the jewelry business: if you don't know your jewels, know your jeweler. The same advice applies to stamp dealers: if you can't verify the authenticity or soundness of a stamp or cover, buy it from a reliable source who will guarantee it or give you your money back.

The most respected stamp dealer's organization in the United States is:

American Stamp Dealers Association
5 Dakota Drive, Suite 102
Lake Success, New York 11042

The ASDA membership list is public information, and you can send a self-addressed stamped envelope to them, asking about the standing of a dealer with whom you are considering doing business. The ASDA has a code of ethics which all members are required to uphold or risk being expelled from the organization. Membership in the ASDA doesn't insure that a dealer is legitimate, and many dealers don't belong for one reason or another (money, philosophy, etc.), but if a dealer is an ASDA member it is one indication that you may be dealing with a fair business person.

You can also check the Better Business Bureau of the city where the stamp company is located to see if it is a firm in good standing. Finally you might ask other stamp collectors what they think of a dealer; they'll often give you an honest opinion. Major dealers who have been around for a while are well known to each other, even if they live in different parts of the country, because the stamp trade is relatively small and close knit. Many dealers do a large part of their business with other dealers, supplying each other with items that their respective customers need.

A precaution to take when buying any expensive stamp is to examine it in good lighting. Natural skylight is window light from the outside, without direct sun rays. Skylight is good for looking at stamps and covers on a cloudless day. Normal incandescent household light bulbs are adequate for lighting stamps under magnifying glasses. Fluorescent light should never be used because it is too blue and makes stamps look pale, and doesn't show defects well.

Determine when buying stamps if you can get a refund if the stamp later turns out to be counterfeit. Find out also if the dealer is willing to buy the same material that he is selling to you. If it is such a good deal, would he like to buy some at half the price he is selling it for? If not, why not?

And you shouldn't buy an expensive stamp until you have comparison-shopped around among several dealers. Legitimate business people aren't afraid of their competition.

NEW ISSUE SERVICES

Some dealers and many overseas countries will accept a cash deposit against future shipments to you of new issues of a particular country or group of countries. You can request just mint singles or blocks or first day covers of each new stamp as it comes out. This way you won't miss any new stamps and your collection will be complete from the day you sign up.

WANT LISTS

Many dealers handle want lists. You give them a written list of the stamps that you seek, arranged by country, mint or used, your condition requirements (fine or superb?), and other special needs (big margins, defects are acceptable at bargain prices, etc.). Then when the dealer has such material in stock he will show it to you either in person or by mail on approval. It is considered unfair to give the same want list to many dealers and shop around for the best prices on cheap stamps, because their time is worth something to them. If they find out you are doing this to save a few cents, they may no longer accept your want lists.

SALES CIRCUITS

One advantage of being a member of a national stamp collecting organization (see Chapter 11) is the sales circuits they may have. They will send you stamps mounted in books. You select the ones you want at the prices indicated and return the balance with your payment to society headquarters. Sales circuits often have unusual material at reasonable prices to members.

AUCTIONS   Auctions are great ways to buy and sell stamps. Some stamp auction houses specialize in material from certain countries or are known for having items in a certain price range.

You can bid by mail or telephone in many auction sales, although a phone bid requires written confirmation as soon as possible. On the day of the scheduled auction, you can bid in person in the hotel or gallery where it is held.

Rules vary from company to company, but in general a public floor stamp auction will sell a group of stamps or covers (known as a "lot") to the highest bidder at a slight advance over the second highest bid. For example, if the highest mail bidder has sent in a bid of $45 for lot number 416, a group of Canadian plate blocks, and you are the only floor bidder present who would like to bid on the lot in person, you can have it for maybe $50, depending on the set increments which the auctioneer establishes for each bid advance.

The beauty of auctions is that stamps achieve their true market values based on consumer supply and demand. The disadvantages of auctions are: a bidder can get carried away in the emotional excitement and bid more than a lot is actually worth; and a seller (known as a consignor) may not get much money for unpopular material because in the open market of the auction no bidders materialize.

Several of the largest and best known stamp auction companies are listed below. They will send you a sample catalog if you write and enclose $3, asking for a recent or forthcoming catalog.

On the East Coast:
>   Robert A. Siegel Auction Galleries
>   160 East 56th Street
>   New York, NY 10022

In the Midwest:
>   Rasdale Stamp Company
>   36 South State Street
>   Chicago, IL 60603

On the West Coast:
>   Superior Stamp & Coin Company
>   9478 West Olympic Boulevard
>   Beverly Hills, CA 90212

and
>   Richard Wolffers, Inc.
>   133 Kearny Street
>   San Francisco, CA 94108

I have no financial interest in any of these companies, but I have dealt with all of them over the last fifteen years and have been satisfied with their business ethics.

One more thing: when you bid in person at an auction you are expected to pay for the lots won on the spot. When you bid by mail you may be asked to send in your payment before the lots are shipped (at your expense).

MAIL BID SALES Don't confuse public auctions with mail sales. A true auction will have floor action — live bidders present during the "crying" of the sale by the auctioneer. A mail bid sale is just that: a catalog, sometimes with illustrations, sometimes without, which lists the lots to be sold to the highest mail bidder, with no actual floor auction to take place.

Mail bid sales all have different rules, so it is smart to get the mail sale company's catalog and read the terms of sale. Often it will say that you cannot return a stamp because of centering if it is pictured in the catalog's illustrations. And mail sales typically state that lots will be sold to the *highest bidder* (not to the highest bidder at one advance over the second highest bid as in true floor auctions).

For example, in a real auction with public attendance, a stamp may rise in bidding prices like this: opening at $100, next bidder says $110, then $120, $130, $140, and sold at $150 with no further bidders speaking up. The high bid of $150 may be a floor bid from a live bidder or a mail bid which no floor bidder is willing to exceed. If it sells to a mail bidder it is called "sold to order" or "sold to the book."

But in a mail bid sale the second highest bid might be $100, while your bid is $150. In that case, you will have to pay the full $150, while in a public auction the auctioneer would lower your top bid to $110 (the first advance over $100) and ask the floor if there are any more bids. If there aren't, you win the lot for $110.

So you see that mail sales can be more expensive than a floor auction if you bid extravagantly. Also, some mail bid sales have been known to misdescribe or overgrade stamps more often than the average auction firm, but most mail bid companies are honest and ethical.

My advice is to send in a small sample bid and see if you like the service and the stamps that you happen to win at either auction or mail sale. If you are satisfied with the company, send in larger bids for more expensive lots.

And if you are consigning your own stamps to be sold in an auction or mail sale, expect to wait two months or more from the date of the sale to get your money. Most companies first collect from the buyers before they pay the sellers (consignors).

The standard auction commission in the United States is ten percent of the selling price to be paid by the seller. The buyer pays another ten percent on top of his bids, giving the auction company its commission for being the "middle man" in uniting seller and buyer.

DIRECT SALE BETWEEN COLLECTORS

You can sell or buy stamps directly if you can contact a stamp collector either by telephone or mail. The stamp weeklies (see Chapter 12) provide classified ad columns for common collectors as well as specialists and investors to advertise their desire to buy or sell specific material.

The advantage of selling directly to another private party is that you may be able to get a higher price than if you sold to a dealer who must put a markup on the material to make a profit. The disadvantage of selling directly is that there is a chance of getting an insufficient funds check or of making your customer mad for some reason and having to handle those problems.

An advantage of buying directly from another collector is that you could get a bargain; a collection or set of stamps cheaper than you would pay at auction or retail. A disadvantage is that you could get burned with counterfeit or repaired merchandise. Will the seller still be there five years from now if you later discover that the stamps you bought from him aren't genuine?

Also there is an opportunity for theft in an expensive transaction between two private parties. It is safer to buy and sell in a stamp shop or to mail stamps by insured parcel.

PRIVATE TREATY

A person can give a stamp or collection to a dealer to sell for him at a predetermined rate of commission. The sale may be for walk-in traffic in a city stamp store, or could be placed in a price list or direct private treaty sale catalog which the dealer sends out to his customers.

A benefit of private treaty is that you can leisurely buy material without feeling the pressure of auction tension, at a price that is set and stable. You can give a dealer a want list of stamps that you would like to buy if the price is right, and he will be on the lookout for your needs, and act as a private treaty broker between a vendor and you.

Private treaty also promotes confidentiality for both buyer and seller. Only three people need to know about the transaction: vendor, dealer, and buyer.

RETAIL PRICE LISTS

Much stamp business is done via printed price lists periodically issued by dealers offering to sell stamps at fixed prices. Prices tend to be a bit higher than at auction, but many cheaper sets or unusual and rare items are sold daily by price list. Price list dealers regularly advertise their lists in the stamp weeklies (Chapter 12).

WHOLESALE LISTS

Wholesale and bulk lots are available to qualified buyers at a discount from normal retail prices. Some dealers cater exclusively to other proven dealers. Some will sell at what is essentially "wholesale" price to anyone with the money.

The most established wholesale stamp publication in the United States is:

> *The Stamp Wholesaler*
> P.O. Box 706
> Albany, OR 97321

Subscription rates are $16.90 per year, $29.80 for two years. Foreign countries add $10 per year for surface mail. Write for air mail rates.

The Stamp Wholesaler has dealer-oriented articles and many classified and display ads geared toward the stamp dealer and bulk investor. Send $1 for a sample copy.

MARKET PRICES

What is a fair price for a stamp? A rough rule is about half retail for wholesale price. If a stamp costs a dealer $25 to buy, he might expect to get about $50 when he sells it.

Or from the other point of view, anticipate paying double the price when buying a stamp when compared with the price at which you could sell it back to the same dealer later that day.

But there are many exceptions. Cheap, common, or slow-moving material may be expensive at ten percent of catalog value, and a dealer might make a large spread between wholesale and retail price for these items.

Stamps that are in high demand and consequently easy to sell may have a wholesale-retail price difference of only ten to fifteen percent (example: buying a set of U.S. Graf Zeppelins at $2000, selling them at $2200).

Remember that a stamp dealer makes money from rapid turnover, not from keeping stamps in stock year after year with no buyers showing up.

Market prices also fluctuate over many months for every reason imaginable: collecting fads, countries in the news, panic (like the stock market), and normal cycles of boom and bust in the psychology of stamp investors' predictions about what will happen in the near future. Nobody can guarantee what a stamp will be worth next year, but there are ways to minimize risks (Chapter 8).

CATALOG VALUES

Nothing in stamp collecting and investing is more misunderstood by neophytes than catalog values.

The stamp catalogs are only a basic guide to prices. Scott's catalogs are edited months in advance of actual distribution. The market can change abruptly in that interval of time, not to mention that the catalog listing for each country's stamps is formally updated with a new catalog only once a year.

A cheap, common stamp may be expensive at half catalog price. A superb one-of-a-kind rarity in heavy demand may be a bargain at triple catalog valuation.

Use the catalog to get a rough idea of what a stamp is worth, not as a bible of true market values. A recent auction results realization sheet or a current dealer's price list is a more accurate gauge of market prices than last year's outdated catalog.

As a general rule, most stamps are sold below catalog value at their retail prices. This is a long established custom which I guess has something to do with collectors wanting to get a good deal when they buy stamps at what seems to be "below catalog" value. In reality, it is an honest retail price with a lower value than the artificially high catalog quotation.

11. Two Union patriotics, Civil War envelopes. Used by citizens to voice their support for the Union cause.

12. Six cent Lincoln large margins regular issue of 1873 with prominent New York City Foreign Mail cancel unlisted in Scott's catalog for this issue. Catalog #159.

13. One cent Franklin with jumbo margins. Normal copy catalogs at $1.20 used. Estimated cash value (ECV), which means the estimated auction selling price, is about $100. Large margined U.S. nineteenth century stamps bring premiums over small margined copies. Catalog #182.

ON APPROVAL

Approvals are stamps or covers that are mailed to you by a stamp dealer so that you can choose which ones you would like to buy in the comfort and privacy of your home. Buying on approval allows you to carefully inspect the material for defects without feeling the pressure of having a dealer watching you.

Cheaper selections of stamps (under $20 total) are often sent out without insurance or checking your references. More expensive items usually require that you submit a cash deposit or trade references before the valuable approvals are mailed to you.

SPECIALIST AND GENERAL DEALERS

Some dealers specialize in certain countries (like Finland or China) or topics (Zeppelin mail or polar covers), others handle everything within their business budgets. A specialist dealer can find elusive and scarce material that perfectly fits in your goals of collecting. A general dealer may be able to supply all kinds of material, making him a "one-stop" supply source.

TRANSACTION LOCATIONS

Stamps are usually most expensive when bought or sold in their country of origin. Big city shops have higher prices than small town stamp stores.

Chapter 7

Selling Stamps

The real price of anything is not what you can buy it for, but what you can sell it for. Things are easy to buy, and there are all kinds of vendors and promoters eager to take your hard-earned money. But try to sell something back to them or to another person and see how excited they get.

Many stamp collectors and investors get angry and discouraged when they go to sell their stamps and find out that nobody wants them, or they want them but at a rock bottom price. Market demand, up and down cycles, the condition of the stamps, and the financial situation of the buyer all influence the inclination to buy or not to buy.

REASONS FOR SELLING

Unless they are donated to a museum or library for public display or research, all stamp collections are eventually sold. We sell to earn instant cash to pay everyday bills; a stamp collection that is worth some money is tempting to raid when we're broke.

We sell when we lose interest in a particular collection or specialty. We outgrow general and poor collections built up over the years, and decide to sell them for ready cash to sink into a more logical and serious branch of philately.

We sell to turn a profit on a short or long term investment; we sell stamps to limit a loss when specific stamp investments are dropping in a falling market.

We sell albums and covers because they take up too much space in our homes. We sell stamps when we happen to meet an enthusiastic buyer for material that we thought wasn't valuable.

We sometimes make distress sales to pay emergency expenses in our lives. Happy is the person who has a stamp collection of worth when unexpected bills pop up.

PREPARING THE COLLECTION FOR SALE

Time is important to dealers. Since most stamp sales will be to dealers who have the cash and markets for our stamps, it is smart to do a little homework in preparing a collection for sale before taking it to a dealer for appraisal.

Separate the cheap stamps from the better items. Whether you're selling in person or shipping the collection across the country, make it clear which stamps are relatively inexpensive, and which ones have significant premium value. Dealers aren't mind readers. They are experienced professionals in the stamp trade, but they can't be expected to automatically identify the $100 items hidden in thousands of penny stamps, unless the valuable ones are popular rarities like the Zeppelins or early British and U.S. definitives.

A collection should be sorted out, properly mounted with hinges or placed in stock books. Covers should be arranged in chronological or monetary order, and expensive ones need to be put in protective holders or plastic sleeves (Mylar, polyethylene, etc.).

It is of immense help and makes a dealer happy to be offered a collection that is annotated with catalog numbers and catalog values, either next to the stamps on album pages or separately listed on a sheet of paper. A cover letter or memo indicating the catalog value of the better items will draw a dealer's attention to what is most worth his trouble when he looks over your material.

Also it is a good idea to eliminate damaged or questionable (maybe counterfeit?) stamps from a group that you are trying to sell. A suspicious stamp in the middle of an otherwise nice set will make the whole works suspect.

MARKET CYCLES The lucky thing to do would be to sell at the peak of a market cycle. Stamps go up and down in price, like other freely traded commodities with competition and supply/demand price making. You can never be sure when a market has peaked or bottomed out, but you can easily find which way it has been heading for the past year or so.

Read market analysis articles in the stamp weeklies (Chapter 12). Save and compare price lists and auction prices realized lists from stamp dealers so that you can personally chart the general price trend of stamps that interest you.

In the 1960s and early 1970s, stamp prices progressed at an orderly and moderate pace. Many exceptions of course existed, but the pattern was for most stamps to be worth a little more every year if they were popular and scarce or semi-scarce items.

Five percent increase per year was considered a good appreciation on a stamp investment at that time period.

In the mid-1970s the market heated up a bit, with gold ownership made legal and the acquisition of speculative collectibles becoming more and more common. Around 1979 through 1981 the prices of certain stamps went through the roof, making them ripe for a price crash.

For example, I remember a set of U.S. Graf Zeppelins bringing near $10,000 at auction in the late 1970s. Current Scott catalog value is $3050 for the Zeppelin set of three (catalog numbers C13-C15), and a set would have to be quite nice to bring that price.

Since 1980 the stamp market has been in decline, but it could start rising at any moment, and many stamps are now selling at bargain prices in the opinion of many qualified observers. If inflation should rise in the 1990s, stamps would once again be appealing to serious speculators and investors, and prices could skyrocket for rare and desirable items.

APPRAISALS

Any stamp dealer will be happy to appraise a collection. Most will offer an informal appraisal for free if you show them some stamps and ask what they are worth. Without naming a specific price, a dealer typically will reply, "I see no value here." Or something like "This collection looks like it is worth some money. Would you like to talk about selling it to me?"

Detailed appraisals requiring time-consuming examination of a large collection, with a written formal evaluation, cost money. Average fees range from two percent to five percent of the appraised value, and should be agreed upon before authorizing the dealer to appraise the stamps.

It is unnecessary to remain with your stamps while they are being appraised, and many dealers prefer to do this work away from their shops, where they can concentrate without being interrupted. No long-established dealer would risk his reputation by stealing stamps from a collection being appraised. And if you have any qualms about leaving valuable stamps with a dealer overnight, take photocopies of them (don't leave them in the machine too long to avoid heat damage), and make a list of valuable items before you give the stamps for appraisal.

Dealers usually waive their appraisal fee if you should sell the collection to them after appraisal.

There are different kinds of appraisals. Why are you getting your stamps appraised? Do you want to know what price they can be expected to bring at auction? How much it would cost to replace them at retail? How much would the dealer buy them for on the spot (wholesale price)? Do you want to know total catalog value? Total value for an insurance policy?

14. One dollar Trans-Mississippi Exposition commemorative (Western Cattle in Storm) issued June 17, 1898. Catalog value $1850 mint. Catalog #292.

15. Thirty cent Reissue of 1875. Not intended to be used as postage. Issued for the Centennial of the U.S. Independence celebration. Catalog value $1000 used. Catalog #131.

16. Ninety cent Lincoln. Used on high postage overseas mail. Earliest known use May 10, 1869. Rare on cover. Catalog value $7000 mint. Catalog #122.

17. Graf Zeppelin set. Issue April 19, 1930 (withdrawn from sale June 30, 1930). Catalog value for the set: $3050 mint. Catalog #C13-C15.

Tell the dealer why you are having your stamps appraised so he knows which of the above prices to put on them. Also, most dealers will be happy to glance at a collection first in order to decide if it is worth appraising at all. It wouldn't make sense to spend $50 to have a collection worth $10 appraised!

SELLING AT AUCTION

My experience has been that auctions determine the true value of stamps. It occasionally happens that a "sleeper" surfaces at auction — an extremely valuable stamp that nobody recognizes except for one bidder who gets it for a ridiculously low bid. And material that may have cost the seller a lot of money may have no takers at an auction, resulting in a disastrously low selling price.

In Chapter 6 I mentioned specific auction firms which are known for fair dealing and reliability when you buy stamps from them. The same advice also applies if you wish to consign stamps to them for sale in their next auction.

Expect to wait a few months after the auction to get your money when you sell at auction. And if you are worried about obtaining too low a price for your stamps, many auction houses allow the seller to put a "reserve" on an auction lot, a minimum price that must be bid or the lot will be returned to its original owner. Sometimes you will be charged a fee for reserved lots that go unsold, however.

The consignor pays the auction company ten percent of the bid price as the company's commission. The buyer also pays ten percent on top of the bid price. For particularly costly stamps or a large valuable collection, an auctioneer will sometimes waive his normal commission in order to get the opportunity to handle such a nice property. In other words, you can negotiate the auction fee down from ten percent to maybe five percent or less.

It is crucial to select the right auction house when you wish to auction stamps. Some companies sell stamps of the whole world, some specialize in rarities, some cater to the beginner and intermediate collector, others sell only certain countries. Ask them what they sell, and get a copy or two of their latest catalogs to see if your material will fit in their business.

My practice is to give a company a sample group of stamps or covers to auction off, wait until the sale is over, and see if I am pleased with the results — both in the amount of money realized and in the service I get from the company. Suppose you are happy with the $600 worth of stamps that a company has sold for you? Consider them for your $3000 collection when the time comes to sell.

DIRECT SALE   There is nothing like the quick cash or check handed to you in a stamp dealer's shop. You get it on the spot, no questions asked. If you are familiar with the kind of material that a local dealer will buy, then all it takes is a trip to his store with your stamps in a bag for his inspection.

Disadvantages of direct sale at a single shop are: he may be closed when you get there for whatever reason; he may be overstocked or undercapitalized at the moment; the dealer might offer you much less than you feel is fair for the collection.

A better solution for direct sale sometimes is to go to a stamp show or bourse. Show schedules are listed every week in the major stamp periodicals (Chapter 12). Find out when the next show will be in your area and take the stamps you want to sell. There will be maybe dozens of dealers with booths at the show, so you can shop around for the best price.

If the collection warrants travel, you should consider waiting for a major show in another city and going there to offer your expensive collection to high-paying dealers from around the country.

PRIVATE TREATY   As mentioned in Chapter 6, private treaty is a system whereby you leave stamps with a dealer at a predetermined selling price, and he tries to sell them for you at an agreed upon fee for his service. This method is good for highly specialized or obscure collections that would interest only a select few collectors. By consigning to private treaty you allow a dealer to wait until the right buyer shows up, someone who is willing to pay a better price than just anybody off the street who knows nothing about the collection's meaning.

A problem with private treaty is that you may wait a long time before the stamps are sold. Direct sale, either by mail to a dealer or over the counter in a shop, brings direct cash.

CLASSIFIED ADS   Inserting a classified ad in one of the philatelic weeklies can bring inquiries to your mailbox about the stamps you are selling. You run the risk though of time-consuming correspondence from collectors who want a pen pal more than they want to buy your stamps. Other potential problems include possible bounced checks, and the difficulty of settling a dispute about the transaction if the buyer lives in another state.

Cheaper material is a prime candidate for classified ads. I once sold a lot of inexpensive U.S. three cent plate blocks by classified ad. I also buy once in a while by classified ad. For five or ten dollars you can insert a short ad in a couple of weeks' issues of the periodical.

Some precautions with classified advertising: sending stamps to a post office box sometimes gives them to a "fly-by-night" crook who skips town without paying. If you answer another person's ad, make it clear in your first letter what specific business you want to transact to head off misunderstandings early. An ad inserted just once by a stranger is always a bit suspicious; it may be perfectly legitimate or it may be a business fraud designed to get free money or stamps.

SELLING TO FOREIGN ADDRESSES

There is nothing wrong with shipping stamps overseas. Stamps sell best in their country of origin if a reasonable number of its citizens have disposable income for stamp collecting and investing.

Insurance rules vary, so ask your post office how much you can insure or register a package for when it is going to a certain country. Pack it well and be sure to enclose a detailed list of contents by catalog number and catalog value.

Air mail overseas averages a week to go one way. That's two weeks for a round trip air mail communication. Be patient when dealing by foreign air mail.

Probably the safest foreign dealers to send stamps to are those who advertise regularly in American stamp magazines, especially if they say "Buying" in their ads. It is always wise to write first before sending stamps to see if they are interested in what you have to sell.

Not all foreign dealers are members of the American philatelic organizations like the American Stamp Dealer's Association (ASDA) or the American Philatelic Society (APS), but there is an address you can write to verify their business ethics: the Philatelic Trader's Society (PTS) is a worldwide organization of stamp dealers in sixty-five countries. Enclosing an American dollar with your inquiry should bring a response about whether or not they know about a few dealers' business practices:

Philatelic Trader's Society
27 John Adams Street
London, WC2N 6HZ, England

Some final selling advice: sell your cheapest and poorest quality material first, keeping the best stuff until you absolutely have to sell it. This is known as "weeding out" and "upgrading" your collection.

Distress sales to obtain emergency money are always dangerous. If you can wait a little to shop around for a better price, you'll be happier with selling stamps.

And if you get good service, by all means sell again and again to that place! If it is a dealer who is eager to buy, he'll often buy material that he doesn't especially want just to keep you as a good source customer.

Chapter 8

Investments

Stamps have been good investments over the past thirty years. Since the mid-1950s, many issues have gone up at a rate that has exceeded the normal rate of inflation.

On the other hand, some stamps have not performed well compared with savings account bank interest. So let's examine the record to understand the factors that make a stamp a potential good investment.

COUNTRIES   Popular countries include those which have a large number of native collectors to support a local demand for their own stamps. Examples: the United States, Great Britain, France, West Germany, Switzerland, and Japan. Choice rare mint or used stamps from any of these places have a ready market in their native lands primarily, and in other prosperous countries abroad.

Because modern mail allows the free transmission of insured parcels between countries, a thriving market exists for choice stamps in the civilized industrial nations. British Penny Blacks (Great Britain #1) can be bought and sold in Paris or Chicago. Japanese souvenir sheets find a home with Swiss investors.

Italy, the Scandinavian nations, Mexico, Hong Kong, Greenland, Iceland, mainland China, Taiwan, Australia, and New Zealand are not as popular as Britain or the United States, but have their enthusiasts and philatelic specialists' societies.

Obsolete countries like the Confederate States of America, pre-confederation Canadian provinces like Newfoundland and Nova Scotia, and early Russian high values are generally easy to sell.

The stamp-issuing policy of a country also influences its popularity among philatelists. Countries like Belgium which has issued about 2500 major varieties of stamps since its first in 1849 tend to have a greater collector following than, say, Romania which has produced over 4000 varieties since 1858. Serious investors are attracted to conservative postal administrations which don't flood the market with "wallpaper," a derogatory term meaning unnecessary stamp issues made solely to get money from collectors.

Of course there are certain issues that have been profitable to investors who have bought Communist stamps, Third World wallpaper, and the proliferating emissions of obscure island governments. But in general, the stamps of the United States, western Europe, and Japan have been better investments, not to mention that they are readily recognized by dealers and are therefore easy to sell.

A country temporarily in the news is not always a good investment. There was a little flurry of demand for Falkland Islands stamps shortly after the war there between Britain and Argentina, but collector interest in Falkland material doesn't seem to be much greater or less at present than it would have been if that conflict had never happened. Expensive Falklands stamps are prime items, by the way, as are many of the present and former European colonies overseas.

Some small nations have wild price swings up and down over the years as investors drive the prices up and then panic and dump their stamps on the market, creating alternating boom and bust cycles. Examples: Vatican City, the United Nations, Monaco.

MINT U.S. STAMP INVESTMENTS

If you are buying full panes (sheets) of new stamps at the post office every month, you are supporting the Postal Service with an interest-free loan, not seriously investing in stamps. With only a couple of exceptions (like the Space Twins issue, Scott U.S. #1331-1332; and the $1 Airlift stamp of 1968, catalog #1341), mint U.S. stamps produced since World War II have been awful investments. Many full panes of stamps of the last forty years are still worth only face value because they were printed in such large quantities. So-called "investors" often are shocked when they take their hoard of mint panes to a stamp dealer who sadly informs them that their imagined treasures are more or less worthless.

Many cheap stamps (under $5 each) have gone up in value over the years, but let's look at the more valuable ones as well to see how they have fared since 1962. Refer to the charts on page 83 for a catalog survey of a dozen selected popular U.S. issues. Notice how prices changed from decade to decade, as well as relative to other issues.

U.S. #1, the five cent Franklin of 1847, a stamp in extreme demand when in nice condition, was listed at $110 mint in 1962 and at $350 in 1971, tripling in value in ten years during what was then an orderly market. But look what happened from 1971 to 1981: $350 to $4500 for the same stamp, the 1981 price being almost *thirteen times* the 1971 quote. Clearly anyone buying a U.S. #1 in 1971 and holding it for ten years made a nice profit.

But the stamp market as a whole peaked in 1980-81, with a gradual decline since then. So U.S. #1 mint quoted at $4500 in 1981 is *still* $4500 in the 1988 catalog. Not a single mint stamp on this chart is worth more in 1988 than it was in 1981, and most have dropped in price.

We've been experiencing a falling market since 1980, due to price run-ups by overzealous buyers in the late 1970s and the general inflationary mood of the entire economy during that time period. Inflation has been at rock bottom in the 1980s, stamp prices included.

Another lesson to be learned from this is that stamps can go down as well as up in price. And a stamp that is overgraded, overpriced, misdescribed, counterfeit, or sold as a sound copy when in fact it has been secretly repaired — such a stamp is a bad investment more times than not! The Postal Inspection Service says that if it looks too good to be true it probably is.

Let's try the same stamp in cancelled condition. On page 83 you see that it is $37.50 in 1962, not quite doubling in value to $65 by 1971. In mint form it tripled in value in those nine years, following a basic rule that rare mint stamps tend to increase in value faster than used examples of the same issue.

A large jump to $825 in 1981 and a drop (charitably called a "price correction" by stamp market analysts) to $700 in 1988 completes the record for #1 used.

There is another reason why stamp prices have stagnated in the 1980s. Investors who got burned left the stamp market for good. Many dealers who were in business in 1980 have closed their doors voluntarily or gone bankrupt since then. It is tough to make money in a falling market.

For instance, many collectors and investors bought the famous Graf Zeppelins (#C13-15) at the market peak around 1979-80 and sold at a disastrous loss a few years later. The charts show #C13-15 at $5500 mint, $3100 used in 1981. Seven years later those prices are $3050 mint, $1625 used, almost half of their 1981 values.

On the other hand, the Zeppelins increased greatly from 1971 to 1981 ($610 to $5500 mint; $397.50 to $3100 used). A person who bought a few Zeppelin sets in 1971, even at double catalog value, probably made a fine profit if they were sold at auction in 1981 (assuming top quality, undamaged stamps, of course!).

For collectors on a more limited budget, the Baby Zeppelin, Scott #C18 issued in 1933 in a quantity of 324,070 (small for an air mail issue) has been a financial substitute for the more expensive Graf Zeppelins. We see that #C18 catalogs $13 mint in 1962, advancing to $50 in 1971, a fivefold increase to $250 in 1981, and a crash to half that, $125, by 1988.

So is it a good investment or not? That depends on when you bought it. The Baby Zeppelin purchased in the mid-1960s and held until 1980 yielded a handsome profit. One bought in 1980 at top market price and held to the present has been disappointing.

Is today a good time to buy U.S. stamps? Like the stock market, the stamp business has its short term and long term cycles. Should inflation in the 1990s heat up again, making collectibles and "hard" assets once more appealing to worried investors, stamps could go through the roof.

But not *every* stamp. After all, investors go for the blue chip items when they put out substantial funds. Carefully chosen rare U.S. and foreign stamps at appropriate late 1980s prices seem to be as good an investment as other things that are being pushed on the public (silver, gold, rare coins, art, etc.). And stamps have the advantage of being easy to store, conceal, ship, and mail.

STAMPS VERSUS OTHER COLLECTIBLES

Why stamps?

1. They are readily recognized for their value by any well-established dealer in any country in the world. Try selling a Korean autograph to a small town bookshop in southern Italy. You probably wouldn't get very far. It would be an unusually ignorant stamp dealer who couldn't identify the leading rarities and investment stamps that are heavily traded around the world.

2. Stamps are compact. Just try stuffing an antique table and chairs into your wallet. How much space do you need to store a

SCOTT CATALOG VALUES
OF SELECTED UNITED STATES STAMPS

CATALOG NUMBER	1962	1971	1981	1988
1	$37.50	$65.00	$825.00	$700.00
2	110.00	200.	2500.00	2000.00
73	3.25	7.00	20.00	20.00
230	.10	.20	.25	.30
245	120.00	350.00	1200.00	1700.00
537	1.10	1.90	4.25	4.25
834	1.25	1.45	5.50	5.50
1053	1.25	1.65	4.50	8.00
C1-C3	22.50	49.50	125.00	162.50
C13-C15	185.00	397.50	3100.00	1625.00
C18	12.00	32.50	127.00	95.00
C31 plate block	5.50	15.00	25.00	unpriced

SCOTT CATALOG VALUES
OF SELECTED MINT UNITED STATES STAMPS

CATALOG NUMBER	1962	1971	1981	1988
1	$110.00	$350.00	$4500.00	$4500.00
2	325.00	1600.00	20,000.00	18,500.00
73	11.00	30.00	100.00	100.00
230	1.60	4.50	27.50	22.50
245	135.00	550.00	4000.00	3600.00
537	1.90	3.50	13.00	11.00
834	10.00	20.00	225.00	125.00
1053	10.00	16.00	150.00	100.00
C1-C3	32.00	86.00	775.00	440.00
C13-C15	260.00	610.00	5500.00	3050.00
C18	13.00	50.00	250.00	125.00
C31 plate block	9.00	40.00	200.00	100.00

collection of classic automobiles? How heavy is a sack of gold or silver bars? A million dollars in rare stamps can easily be concealed in your closed hand (carefully closed, of course, so you don't damage the paper of the stamps which should be in protective mounts anyway).

3. Safe deposit box convenience makes stamps a good investment. As an extension of their smallness, stamps can be saved by the hundreds in the smallest-sized bank safe deposit box. Can you get an oil painting or a Ming vase into your present box?

4. Insurance is relatively cheap and easy to obtain for the average stamp collection (see Chapter 10). How does one go about insuring a stable of racehorses or a kitchen full of expensive china and silver? Stamps are easy to appraise and insure.

5. Transport. A house or apartment building has to be legally sold in order to be liquidated. A stamp collection can be stuffed in a piece of luggage and flown to anyplace on Earth and sold there. When Hitler invaded the landscape of Europe, many people escaped from Nazi oppression by hiding their stamp collections in their clothes or luggage and thereby sneaking out something of value that they could sell to begin a new life elsewhere.

If war broke out today, and enemy soldiers were fifty miles away, do you think you could get a good price for the family farm? If you have an envelope of rare stamps you could grab them and run.

6. Standard catalogs and endless price lists make stamps easy to appraise. How do you appraise a box of diamonds, each one unique in size, quality, and cut? I can tell you within maybe twenty percent either way of my estimate what many stamps will bring either at auction, at wholesale dealer buying price, or at retail. A piece of handmade jewelry is unique; an ancient Greek sculpture is awesome but has an intangible price. A stamp's value is somewhat stable and commonly agreed upon at any point in time.

In fact, many dealers advertise specific buying prices at which they will buy stamps in stated conditions: very fine mint, no hinge, etc. When was the last time you saw an antique shop advertising: "Wanted to buy: Chippendale chairs. $5000 superb, $3460 fine, $2284 with worm holes. Cash on delivery."

WHAT NOT TO BUY The most important thing to know when deciding to invest money is what not to buy. There is no guarantee that the stuff with a proven track record will continue to appreciate in value in the future. But there is plenty of evidence that certain philatelic material is almost certain to go nowhere financially. For example:

1. First day covers at $3 apiece. Sure, many early first days are worth much more, but the majority of United States first day covers of the last forty years can be bought for less than fifty cents each. You'll see big ads in non-philatelic publications promoting first day covers in special albums, with certificates authenticating them, all for $3 or so per cover. These are always poor investments.

2. Mint panes (sheets) of stamps from the post office. Modern U.S. commemoratives have press runs of 150 million or more, enough to satisfy every collector in the country. Recent U.S. stamps, with a few exceptions, are notoriously poor investments.

3. Overpriced material. Shop around to see what other dealers are charging for the *same* material in the *same* condition. Overpriced items make poor investments.

4. Certain errors are not as rare or valuable as they are advertised. To find out what an error is really worth, call up a few dealers who aren't selling the item and ask what they would be willing to pay for it. If their buying price is a mere fraction of another dealer's selling price, pass it up for something better.

5. Cancelled-to-Order (CTO) junk. When a foreign government's postal officials want to make some fast money for their government without giving postal service in exchange, they sometimes make cancelled-to-order stamps and sell them at a discount to wholesalers, who in turn sell to local dealers and ultimately to the common collector. CTO material is typically cancelled neatly on the corners of the stamps in large sheets, with cancels that are too perfect, or at least look suspiciously different from normal post office business cancels. Ask any dealer to show you some CTO stuff, and memorize what it looks like so you can avoid it.

Better yet, if you don't believe me, just call up or visit any stamp dealer and tell him that you have lots of CTO material that you want to sell, and watch the expression on his face.

6. Communist, Third World, and "sand dune" junk. This is also known as *wallpaper* in stamp slang. Communist and poor countries have their assets and noble achievements, but

manufacturing investment-quality stamps since World War II isn't one of them. Of course there are exceptional stamp issues from Russia, poor African states, etc., that have gone up in price since they were released in the last quarter century, but most have been poor investments.

7. Large collections of cheap stamps that are hard to sell. It may be appealing to see a collection of 50,000 stamps for sale at ten percent of catalog value, but what are you getting? If it is such a great deal, why can't they get even half catalog value? And if they're advertising it and begging people to buy it, can it be worth buying? Cheap stamps are stamps costing less than $1 each, and those costing pennies each are hardly the thing that other collectors seek, so why invest in them?

8. Common covers at less than $1 each. At the present time, you can buy first day covers from any stamp dealer (at least the ethical ones!) for less than $1 apiece for common varieties. Tell me how these covers will put your kids through college, or fly you around the world after you hang onto them for a few years? Covers priced cheaply aren't in demand or they wouldn't be cheap to buy. And if they're not wanted now, why will they be ten years from now?

9. Mixtures and cheap miscellaneous assortments. These are great for beginners to learn how to identify the different countries and time periods of worldwide stamps. They are poor investments for advanced investors. It is quite rare when someone discovers a valuable stamp in a cheap mixture. How did it get there? Why didn't somebody recognize it and isolate it from the common stuff?

10. What dealers themselves don't want to buy. Check with them first and if they don't want to buy it now, why do you suppose they'll come begging for it in the near or far future?

SHORT TERM VERSUS LONG TERM

In my opinion, there is no such thing as a short term stamp investment. Any stamp bought with the intention of holding it for a year or two to turn a nice profit is a stamp bought on speculation. There are price swings in months, but serious investors think in terms of five to ten years when sinking real money into anything worthwhile.

My advice is to buy stamps that appeal to you emotionally for your collection for the short term. For stamps purchased with five to ten years storage in mind, consider these factors:

1. Stamps with a good track record tend to make better investments than "dark horses" which have been the same price for as long as you can remember. Like quality stocks or prime real estate, blue chip stamps may have temporary slumps, but their overall performance is up over many years. Classic nineteenth century U.S. and foreign stamps are better ten year investments than cheap issues priced at less than $1 each — which haven't moved in price in ages.

2. Plan a real collection that is coherent and meaningful. If you intend to be around until the year 2000, then how about laying out a strategy for acquiring all the U.S. air mails in mint, used, and plate block form? Or a complete set of twentieth century Irish issues? Or all the French and British definitives ever issued?

Such collections would have more interest for a buyer than say, a miscellaneous group of covers of the world of all time periods or the same money put into a general world album of medium-priced ($3 to $10 stamps) commemoratives in incomplete sets from fifty different countries.

3. Stick with one or two favorite countries for serious investments. Learn about the particular country and its postal history so you can make wise investment decisions when faced with its rare stamps.

4. Limit yourself to one time period. While a complete run of stamps from start to finish (for example, all major varieties of Egyptian stamps, 1866 to date) has a special beauty, you might want to buy just pre-World War II U.S. special deliveries or postage dues in mint plate blocks, or expensive European souvenir sheets of the 1930s and 1940s.

5. Top condition is important for long term philatelic investments. In a rising market, condition tends to be judged more loosely than in a falling, tight money market. If you always pay close attention to getting the nicest condition that you can possibly afford, then you will have less trouble selling those items in any market time span.

6. Think expensive if you're shooting for a ten to twenty year stamp investment. Instead of buying ten stamps at $10 each, buy one stamp at $100. The $100 stamp may never be cheaper, and very likely will be in demand in the future as it is today. Why is the $10 stamp only priced at $10? Is it because it is much more common and therefore less desirable now than the $100 stamp?

And consider the far distant day when you will liquidate. Would you rather find ten customers or dealers for ten stamps or one buyer for one stamp? Not all dealers appreciate being offered many copies of something they already have in stock, unless they can get it for a bargain price — something not always in the best interest of the investor searching for a buyer.

7. Keep informed on the yearly progress of your stamp portfolio. If some items aren't moving up at all, is it worth keeping them another five years or should you sell them now and sink the money into other stamps?

8. *Look* at your investment once in a while. Long term storage can wreak havoc with stamps susceptible to heat, dust, humidity, and mold damage. Your investment might not be worth anything if you don't watch it over the years and store it properly.

9. Finally, don't invest money you think you'll need next summer. Probably the biggest downfall of investors of any kind is that they can't wait for the eventual upturn in market prices that must come for quality rare stamps with a broad collector demand. It is discouraging to buy a stamp for $100, have to sell it for emergency funds six months later for $60, then see the catalogs list it for $500 years later when you no longer own it!

SPECIAL INVESTMENT ADVICE

1. Buy from established, reliable dealers who guarantee their merchandise.

2. Buy top quality.

3. Buy popular countries like the U.S., Canada, western Europe, and Japan.

4. Buy expensive stamps with low press runs. Scott's *U.S. Specialized* catalog lists the quantities printed for commemoratives and air mails. It is sometimes good sense to buy a stamp that is scarce than a more common one for the same money.

5. Diversify your stamp portfolio a bit. Maybe several different countries, mint as well as used, some choice covers thrown in, and plate number or inscription blocks. That way, you will be spreading the risk around instead of putting all your philatelic money into one area.

6. And don't complain if you're not doubling your money every year. Banks and savings and loan associations offer less than ten percent interest insured by the federal government. Nobody

18. Fifty cent Graf Zeppelin (also called the "Baby Zeppelin") issued October 2, 1933. Catalog value $125 mint. Catalog #C18.

19. Set of C13-C15 First Day Covers, cancelled April 19, 1930 in Washington, DC. Catalog value totalling $5250 on separate covers as shown. If all three stamps were on the same first day cover envelope, the cover catalogs $12,500.

20. Three dollar yellow green Columbian Exposition commemorative (Columbus Describing his Third Voyage) issued January 2, 1893. Catalog value $2600 mint. Catalog #243.

21. Five dollar black Columbian Exposition commemorative (Portrait of Columbus) issued January 2, 1893. Catalog value $3600 mint. Catalog #245.

22. Graf Zeppelin $2.60 plate number block of six. Issue date April 19, 1930. Catalog value $13,000. Catalog #C15.

guarantees any return on stamps, so should you complain if you're not getting rich? If it was that easy, we'd all be rich. Stamps *can* be a good long term investment.

WHAT TO BUY   Or let's title this section "Stamps that I wish I owned!" No human being can foresee the future. But based on past experience in watching the price movements of choice stamps year after year, here are my recommendations for long term stamp investments.

1. Very fine mint or lightly cancelled nineteenth century U.S. stamps, *undamaged*, and with any items costing over $500 coming with official expertizing certificates from the APS or Philatelic Foundation (see Chapter 9). Minimum retail price $50.

2. Early U.S. air mails from Scott numbers C1 through C18, mint or used, very fine centering, no defects, and plate number blocks of the cheaper stamps. Minimum price preferably over $100 per item.

3. Early Great Britain and her present and former colonies, very fine to extremely fine condition, mint and used. Minimum retail price $50.

4. Wells Fargo and other early express company covers. California gold rush covers. Slight defects to be tolerated on items costing over $100. Pony Express mail for investors with over $1000 to spend per cover.

5. U.S. Columbian and Trans-Mississippian stamps, mint and used, nice condition, Scott #230-245 and 285-293.

6. Any U.S. first day cover listed in the Scott catalog for over $200. Get them immaculate without any defects (including dirty areas, creases, off-center stamps).

7. Zeppelin stamps and covers of the world. No defects. Mint or cancelled. On or off cover. Preferably items costing over $100 each, including plate number blocks like U.S. Scott #C18 (listed in the 1988 catalog at $1100 for a plate block of six).

8. Anything expensive (over $100) from the Confederate States of America, Hawaii, or Guam overprints. Buy all these with expertizing certificates when in doubt about their authenticity.

9. U.S. Civil War patriotic covers costing over $100 each when honestly priced. Foreign usage of such covers. Prisoner of war covers from the Civil War. Slight defects to be expected.

10. Major U.S. errors cataloging for over $500 each, especially the inverts like Scott numbers 119b, 294a, and C3a. Quality inverts like these will cost a lot of money, so be careful of minor defects and pay accordingly. Buy only from established major dealers who will not grossly overprice.

11. Encased postage stamps, Scott US #1-181 in the catalog's "back-of-the-book" section. Beware of fakes, including repaired mica and substituted stamps of better condition or of a higher denomination. Get certificates.

12. Expensive foreign stamps, with certificates, if you know what you are doing. Buy from reputable dealers, buy the items that keep appearing at auction (popular!), and watch out for minor defects. Pay less than catalog price except for unusual material.

Chapter 9

Stamp Repairs and Fakes

Many valuable stamps have been repaired or counterfeited to bilk the unwary collector or investor. Some common types of faking and methods of detecting them are discussed in this chapter.

REPERFORATING   The perforations are the tiny holes that are punched between adjacent stamp designs on a sheet to facilitate separating the stamps for postal use. A single stamp has approximately half of a perforation hole alternating with extended projections of paper called the "teeth" of the stamp.

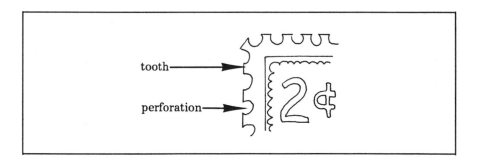

A stamp which has lost its original clean perforations may be fraudulently reperforated along one or more of its sides. Some identifying characteristics of fake perfs are holes that don't match in number or size with the perforations along the rest of the stamp, holes that are too "clean" with teeth too "crisp" for the age of the stamp, and a row of perforations that is out of alignment with the parallel row on the other side. Teeth that seem to be cut rather than torn from the neighboring stamp are also suspect.

A perforation gauge is essential for the serious philatelist. You can buy one at any stamp shop for a dollar or two. It is a small piece of cardboard or a metal strip with standard perforation divisions imprinted, so that the collector can match up any stamp with the printed measurement to determine the stamp's perforation "gauge."

The number of perforations per two centimeters of stamp edge length is that stamp's gauge. For example, a particular issue of U.S. regulars has 14-1/2 perforations per two centimeters along its vertical border, and 15 perfs/2 cm. along its horizontal side. The gauge on the horizontal side is always stated first: 15 by 14-1/2, or 15 x 14-1/2 is the way you write it for this example.

Scott's *Standard Postage Stamp Catalogue* lists the known perforations of all legitimate stamps issued by the world's known countries, so one method of detecting counterfeit perfs is to check the stamp's perforation gauge against its official gauge.

PAPER   The paper of a stamp must be of nearly the same thickness, stiffness, and color as an original. The accepted way to verify paper quality is to compare the suspect item with a stamp that is known to be genuine. This is what expertizing services do when they pass judgment on stamps submitted for their guarantee certificates.

GUM   The glue on the backside of a stamp is called its gum. Herman Herst, Jr., the famous stamp dealer now retired, says that stamp gum is the most valuable thing in the world, even more precious per ounce than uranium or diamonds.

Since World War II, for several strange reasons, collectors and investors have been willing to pay a hefty premium for rare stamps with undamaged original gum when compared with the same issues with slightly disturbed gum. "OG.NH." means "original gum, never hinged," the ultimate in gum freshness, and the basic criterion of serious investors who buy stamps for potential profits.

For example, the fifty cent U.S. air mail issue picturing the Graf Zeppelin (issued October 2, 1933 in New York City), Scott number C18, sells for about $110 in pristine, mint condition, but only about $60 or $65 if the gum has the slightest disturbance from licking, stamp album hinging, or sticking to something since it was sold in the post office.

Collectors in Europe or Israel will often pay three or four times the price for a stamp if it is never-hinged original gum rather than accept a specimen with disturbed gum.

So stamps often have fake gum applied, or the original gum liquified and resmoothed by humidifying the stamp until the gum becomes soft enough to spread over the roughened areas. Dishonest "stamp doctors" have gone as far as to get a quantity of damaged mint stamps of an issue and carefully soak off their gum into a small container. They then apply it on the back of a well-centered stamp of that issue which happens to have no gum remaining, thus giving it a gum composition that is chemically identical to the original gum!

Always compare the gum on a rare stamp with a known genuine example. Gum has a tendency to turn yellow, crack, and become more brittle with age. And different chemical formulas have different aging characteristics. The gum on Spanish stamps from the year 1900 doesn't look like the gum from U.S. stamps of that year.

Distinguishing traits of faked gum: it looks too good or too "new" for the stamp's age. It drips over onto the front of the stamp; genuine stamps have no gum smears on their fronts. The perforation teeth are too stiff, evidence of added gum soaking into their cut fibers. And if the gum looks wavy or in abnormal thicknesses or thin areas on the stamp's back, be suspicious.

TEARS AND HOLES

Tears and holes drastically detract from a stamp's value. It is common to repair a tear or fill a hole so that the stamp appears undamaged. A one millimeter hole or a five millimeter tear in a stamp makes it worthless to discriminating investors, so there is a big incentive to crooks to buy damaged stamps cheaply and repair their tears to sell them later as purported undamaged specimens.

Ultraviolet light will sometimes reveal the lines along which a tear has been glued. Holding a stamp up to a strong light bulb or sunlight will often do the same. Dipping a suspected stamp into watermark fluid, face down in a black ceramic dish, will usually confirm the presence of thin or repaired areas in the stamp's paper.

Any legitimate stamp dealer will let you check a rare stamp in watermark fluid before you buy it, although he may prefer to handle the stamp so that you don't accidentally damage it while dipping. Always use quality fluid and steel stamp tongs for dipping (cost about $6 or $7 total at any stamp shop).

It is legal to sell damaged or repaired stamps as long as they are not misrepresented. The "rarest" stamp in the world, the one cent British Guiana black-on-magenta from 1856 has its four corners torn off. Its last auction price in 1980 was close to $1,000,000. But in general, a torn stamp has its market value slashed.

FAKED INK

Once in a while you run into a stamp that is completely counterfeit, including faked printing ink, or one that has had a scratched-off part of its design redrawn in modern ink that attempts to match the original color. Ultraviolet lamps, watermark fluid tests, dipping in plain tap water, and holding it up to the light are quick tests on suspect ink. Genuine ink should be smooth and without conspicuous light or dark areas in the stamp's design, unless it was originally applied more heavily such as closely engraved lines in a president's head of the U.S. 1938 regular issue series.

Some countries have used "fugitive inks" in stamp printing, ink which dissolves in plain water. The catalogues usually state whether a stamp's ink is fugitive, and any good dealer can tell you if a rare stamp has water-soluble ink and therefore shouldn't be soaked.

Ink fades over the years, especially if exposed to light or air pollution, so you can't always tell by a stamp's shade if the ink is genuine. But a familiarity with the normal run of colors of a particular stamp issue will alert you to an ink shade that doesn't look right.

And beware of chemically altered colors to artificially create a faked shade. Color errors are rare and well known to informed philatelists. Get any color error expertized before you buy it because the color of any stamp can be changed by simple chemical baths. There is sometimes a trace of the chemical present or other incriminating evidence on a color-altered fake that can only be detected in an expertizing laboratory.

FAKED EXPERTIZING CERTIFICATES

These are known to exist, so write to the issuing agency when purchasing an expensive stamp that comes with a certificate if you doubt the certificate's authenticity.

Because it takes many years of experience to be able to distinguish real from faked items in any field of stamp collecting, several prestigious expertizing services have been set up to pass judgment and issue guarantee certificates for rare stamps. These certificates are professional opinions, and may

23. Twenty-four cent Inverted Jenny Airmail issued May 13, 1918. This copy is plate position 3 with a natural straight edge as existed on the top of the pane. Catalog value $120,000 mint. Catalog #C3a.

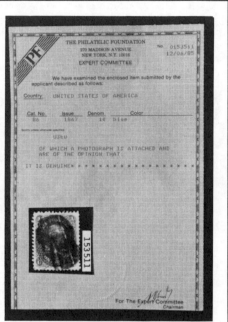

24. Philatelic Foundation Certificate (PFC) declaring that stamp with U.S. catalog #86 is genuine. Catalog value $250. Note the certificate's date: 1985. The more recent the certificate the better because recent knowledge and constant research are always updating our information about rarities. Catalog #86 is the one cent blue "E" Grill.

25. Backside of Z-Grill issue of 1867, Catalog #85E. Catalog value $1550 mint, $550 used.

26. Thirty cent Shield, Eagle & Flags issue in rare block of nine. Issue date May 15, 1869. Unlisted in Scott's. Used block of four alone catalogs $1150. Catalog #121.

sometimes be wrong, but are the best we have at present for insuring relatively honest transactions when buying or selling rare stamps.

Expertizing fees range from about $10 up, depending on the catalog value of the stamp. The certificate will usually come with a photograph of the stamp, a description of its faults if any, the country and catalog number, a statement of whether it is mint or cancelled, and one or more official signatures from executives in the organization.

I recommend getting a certificate if you fear that a stamp might not be genuine in any respect.

For American or foreign stamps, send a stamped, self-addressed number ten (business size) envelope for a form and list of fees to: American Philatelic Expertizing Service, P.O. Box 8000, State College, PA 16803.

For any rare U.S. stamp, the accepted expertizing authority is the Philatelic Foundation, 270 Madison Avenue, New York, NY 10016.

FAKED CANCELLATIONS

Some stamps are more valuable or are unknown with genuine cancels. If a stamp is significantly more valuable with a cancel than it is in mint condition, there is a strong temptation for a forger to fake a cancellation.

Good cancel fakes are extremely difficult to detect. Ultraviolet light and watermark fluid are the first tests, but the forger may

have been clever enough to obtain some cancellation ink that matches the chemical composition of ink cancels of the time period.

Basically, long experience in seeing and handling many stamps with similar cancels is what's needed to pass judgment on the authenticity of a cancel mark. When in doubt, buy from reliable dealers and ask for an expertizing certificate to accompany rare and valuable cancelled items.

If a stamp is on original envelope paper, the cancellation should extend from the stamp to the envelope material to help insure that the stamp hasn't been added later to the envelope to increase its value. This is called "tied on" and is necessary when paying top dollar for cancels on envelopes:

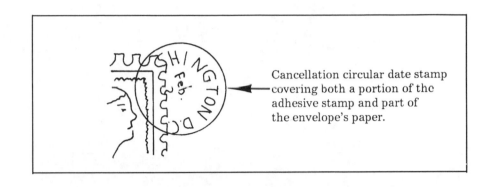

Cancellation circular date stamp covering both a portion of the adhesive stamp and part of the envelope's paper.

If the stamp is on its whole original envelope as used, then the item is called a "cover" and the stamp is listed in price lists or auction catalogs as being properly tied "on cover."

If just the front of the envelope exists with a properly cancelled stamp of the time period, the item is known as "cancelled on envelope front."

If the stamp is cancelled on just a portion of the original envelope remaining, usually the upper right corner of the envelope, it is termed cancelled on piece or "tied to piece" (TTP in auction abbreviation).

It is much easier to fake a cancel on piece than on a whole cover because the rest of the envelope isn't present to incriminate the forger. For example, a high value nineteenth century U.S. stamp (say, ninety cent or one dollar denomination) may be extremely rare and quite expensive when found with an original cancellation. The addresses and other postal markings may indicate that such a high denomination couldn't be used on a local or lightweight envelope, but if all you have is the stamp cancelled on piece, then you can't be sure if the postage use is genuine.

Sometimes postal marks, routing markings, and even addresses are forged on a cover, so the serious collector of old mail must learn what the real items look like. This takes years of study and endless handling of genuine items. When buying or selling rare stamps, if you don't know your stamps, know your stamp dealer.

Chapter 10

Condition

Paper is one of the most fragile substances ever invented. Animal skin vellum parchment documents have survived from the Middle Ages, and pre-Civil War rag content letters often look almost as fresh as the day they were penned.

But stamp papers as we know them are notoriously poor quality, especially twentieth century high sulfur, cheap pulp paper which forms the substrate for many modern postage stamps. What can be done to protect our philatelic gems — not just for future generations, but so that they'll still be okay later in our own lives when we might want to sell them?

PAPER'S ENEMIES There are many enemies of paper, trying their best to destroy the delicate flat sheet from the moment it is dried. Some of these forces are more damaging than others, but if you want to give your stamps and covers the best practical protection within financial and logistical reason, do what you can to reduce the effects of the following:

Heat Paper dries out completely when heated sufficiently to drive off its water content. Desiccated paper becomes brittle and prone to tear and crack. Store stamp collections away from heaters, sunlight, kitchens, and furnaces.

Moisture All papers are manufactured from some sort of paste or pulp before being pressed into the sheets for stamp production. Paper acts like a sponge, absorbing water from the air when it is prevalent, and releasing water to the air when the atmosphere is unusually dry.

Symptoms of excess moisture in stamps are curling, gum sticking to things including other stamps, and after a period of time the worst effects are mold growth (also called "tropical staining" in stamp talk). About fifty percent relative humidity might be right for stamp storage, but this is not always feasible in a home.

To play it safely, keep stamps away from bathrooms, swimming pools, and kitchens with boiling water on the stove. If you live near the beach or a foggy lake, consider buying silica gel or other such desiccant chemical (photography shops often have it) for placing around your collection to absorb moisture.

Water vapor can warp and start fungal growth on stamps. Moisture is sometimes more common in the air than we realize. Keep stamps away from aquariums and dining room areas where steaming food is served. And garages where temperatures can drop a lot at night, causing condensation, are not good places for stamp collections.

Light Direct sunlight is devastating to stamps. The ink fades, the paper fibers weaken, the paper color itself becomes altered in the intense rays of the sun. Look what happens to a newspaper left out in the sun for a few days. If you have stamps in a frame on the wall or cabinet, make certain that the sun never touches them.

And experiments with some fluorescent lights show that prolonged exposure of stamps may result in color fading. The smart thing to do is never keep stamps on permanent display in any kind of light.

Still Air Collections kept locked up where the stamps can't "breathe" or get a little air circulation have a tendency to develop mold or other problems like sticky gum.

Don't seal a stamp or cover in a plastic envelope or a tiny box because any dangerous air conditions near at the time of sealing will be locked in.

Experienced philatelists advise that albums be stored upright, like books on a shelf, and taken down once every few months to examine for any mold or other developing problems. Covers should be mounted on album pages or stored in open clear cover envelopes made of inert material.

Dirt It is amazing how much dust accumulates in the average room. It blows in through the doorways and windows, it is dragged in by shoes and on clothes; it is present on virtually all objects brought into the house and will contaminate your stamps if you give it a chance.

Obvious precautions against dirt are to store stamps above the floor, away from ventilators, away from window openings (did you ever look at a window sill that hasn't been washed in months?), and not on top of a bookcase or cabinet where dust is settling all day long.

And when your albums or stamp boxes get dusty, wipe them off before opening them and wafting the dust on the stamps. And wash your hands before handling rare stamps! Especially if you just ate dinner or were working on your car.

Air Pollution

It is hard to believe how many different sources can pollute the air around our precious stamps. Tobacco smoke, factory fumes, cooking smoke from inside stoves or outside barbecues, paint fumes from your newly-painted hallway, automobile exhaust blowing in the living room window from the driveway, all kinds of chemicals in the air can assault your stamp collection!

Without moving to Antarctica or the moon, we can protect our stamps from flagrant air contaminants by using common sense. Don't smoke around stamps, keep paint, floor cleaners, etc. away from the albums, if you live in a city shut the windows on days of heavy air pollution, and think about which direction fans are blowing and what they're blowing besides air!

Hands

The natural skin oils and salts, plus the day's dirt and assorted adhering chemicals, all get on a stamp when we touch it with bare hands. Expensive stamps should never be handled except with stamp tongs (see Chapter 2). Rare and valuable stamps and covers should be placed in protective clear plastic envelopes or in inert stock books or on approval cards made of safe materials.

Sometimes months after touching a piece of paper you will notice a fingerprint beginning to develop, evidence of skin contaminants on the day it was touched. And freshly washed hands may not be as clean as they look; use stamp tongs if the stamp is important to you. Also, clumsy fingers can damage stamps more easily than proper use of tongs in handling them.

WHERE TO STORE STAMPS

It is fun to have our stamps at home within quick reach when we want to look at them. Burglars know this and the more sophisticated ones are always on the lookout for valuable collectibles like stamps or coins when they break into a house or apartment.

The first places a burglar looks are drawers, bookshelves, and cabinets. Professional burglars search under the beds, in closets, behind pictures, and in boxes or containers that have the potential of yielding valuables.

Don't keep all of your stamps in one location in your home. Don't put them out in plain view, avoid the obvious drawers and shelves, and if you keep high-priced stamps at home, either insure them or consider buying a burglar-proof safe.

Safes   Burglar-proof safes are different from fireproof safes. If the safe is rated as burglar resistant, it should have thick steel walls impervious to simple drills and hammers, a tough combination lock, and be either bolted to the floor or so heavy that it can't be moved without special equipment.

In a sense, no safe is completely burglar proof; a determined thief can dynamite it or blowtorch his way in if he has the expertise and equipment. But a burglar-resistant safe will render your stamps untouchable for the casual burglar.

A fireproof safe may not be burglar proof. Some fireproof safes have walls that are heat resistant, other have water or another chemical that sprays the safe's contents (ruining stamps if present) when the inside temperature reaches a point below the ignition point of paper.

It is wise to avoid storing stamps in a fireproof safe.

Bank Storage   There is nothing like the peace of mind that comes from knowing your stamps are in a bank safe deposit vault. Many vaults these days have controlled temperature and humidity, and are usually better than the best possible home storage facility.

Get a safe deposit box that fits your collection. Store your most expensive items in it. Plastic approval cards fit nicely in even the smallest bank boxes. And remember: safe deposit box contents are rarely insured by the bank. You need to buy insurance from a private company to cover theft or acts of nature (floods, earthquakes, fires, etc.) because banks don't insure their box vault contents.

STAMP INSURANCE   The most convenient stamp insurance is the coverage provided by the American Philatelic Society located at:

APS Insurance Plan
Box 157
Stevenson, MD 21153

They provide insurance for collections kept at home or in bank safe deposit vaults. Typical premiums are $34 per year for $10,000 coverage, $69 per year for $20,000 coverage, etc. Special premium reductions are offered for stamps stored in home safes or bank vaults for coverage in excess of $25,000.

APS members or APS applicants may apply for this insurance. A detailed inventory list is not required, nor is a professional appraisal necessary. Only items valued by the collector at $5000 or more need to be itemized.

APS Insurance Plan *coverage includes* crime, mail loss, exhibition loss, travel, fire, flood, and natural catastrophes.

Not covered are losses from gradual deterioration, handling damage, insects and vermin, dampness, mysterious disappearance of individual items, common carrier transits, unattended auto, checked baggage, numismatic property, government confiscation, war, and nuclear losses.

APS stamp insurance policies are underwritten by Crum & Forster Company, a Xerox corporation subsidiary which has insured stamp collections since 1971.

At probably a greater premium, you can get your own insurance company to write a floater policy to cover your stamp collection, but there are usually appraisal requirements and problems in getting it because of a lack of stamp knowledge by your usual insurance agent.

SAFE ALBUMS   A safe stamp album is one which not only keeps the stamps in some kind of logical order, but also protects them from the elements and from *itself*. Valuable stamps should be mounted in albums made of acid-free paper. It is best to write the album manufacturer and get advice from your stamp dealer because album manufacturers are constantly changing their merchandise so what is acid-free today may not be acid-free tomorrow (or vice versa).

A quality glassine peelable hinge mounting a gumless stamp on an acid-free album page is usually a good way to store stamps. For expensive cancelled or gummed stamps you may want to use an inert plastic mount or stamp sleeve. And whatever album you get, check it at least a couple of times a year to be sure it is really protecting your stamps and not hurting them.

SAFE MOUNTS AND SLEEVES

Many clear plastic mounts, envelopes, pockets, tubes, sleeves, and pages have been developed since World War II for the philatelic accessories market. While it may not matter for short term storage, long term protection of stamps and covers requires some thought and planning.

Hinges are cheap and easy to use, but clear plastic mounts and holders offer the advantages of visibility, gum protection, and theoretical damage-free storage. Pick mounts that fit the size of your items.

Mylar and polyethylene seem to be safe for practical purposes in storing stamps and covers. Plexiglass acrylic plastic holders are great also, as are normal glass sheets for framing displays.

Stay away from translucent (not completely clear) soft mounts with plasticizers or a strong chemical smell. Don't use polyvinyl chloride (PVC), cellophane, discolored plastics, or any material containing sulfur or acids. Many stamps have been ruined after spending a few years in a plastic mount that damaged them chemically.

And it is a good idea to let your plastic-encased stamps breathe. Don't seal the mount on all sides. Corrosive plastic fumes can form in a completely sealed mount, eating away at your treasured stamp or cover.

Don't use any tape around a stamp collection, especially transparent self-adhesive tapes which can permanently stain paper collectibles. Use the normal adhesive provided on the back of a commercial stamp mount to affix it on your album page, or use a stamp hinge.

HANDLING AND MAILING RARE STAMPS

Stamp tongs, glassine envelopes, plastic approval cards and cover sleeves, and safe albums and boxes are needed to handle rare stamps. Handle them as little as possible, however, because you always run the risk of dropping and damaging a rare stamp. They don't move the Mona Lisa every day or constantly touch George Washington's clothes in the Smithsonian.

A large clean flat table or desk with good lighting and proper tongs and stamp holders is a great location for handling stamps. Keep dust and air drafts away so things don't get dirty or blow off onto the floor.

When mailing rare stamps to a dealer for sale, carefully mount them on album pages or wrap them in a stiff plastic approval card, then sandwich them between cardboard sheets. Place them inside a protective packing envelope (preferably manila paper), and insert them into an outer mailing envelope, strong enough to withstand the journey by mail. The whole package should not be easy to bend, as the mails are often roughly handled.

Then the parcel has to be weighed and stamped with sufficient postage. I recommend sending rare stamps by first class registered mail. For around $4 plus postage based on weight you can send hundreds of dollars worth of stamps with complete safety through the U.S. Postal Service. Insurance mailings cost somewhat less, but don't get the attention and protection that registered parcels do. Large or cheap contents should be sent insured instead of registered.

And register or insure your stamps for their full value so that you can be reimbursed should they be lost or damaged in transit.

Chapter 11

National Stamp Societies

Membership in a philatelic society has benefits that far exceed the annual dues which usually run between $10 and $20. A chance to meet other people who are also interested in your specialty area, trading privileges, expertizing services, and the latest published research are certainly worth a dollar or two a month. One fact learned from one issue of a society journal can repay your membership fee many times over.

Nobody will come to your home or beg for extra donations if you join a national stamp society. Most guard their membership lists with special trust, and you may keep your address confidential if you wish. Membership in societies is good for references; a ten year APS or ATA member is looked upon as serious and somewhat creditworthy.

Here are some of the more popular societies. Send a self-addressed stamped envelope for the latest information regarding membership requirements, annual dues, etc.:

1. American Air Mail Society (AAMS), 70-C Fremont Street, Bloomfield, NJ 07003. Local chapters, publishes quality handbooks, exhibition awards. The official publication, *The Airpost Journal*, appears monthly. $12 annual dues.

2. American First Day Cover Society (AFDCS), 203 Village Way, Brick, NJ 08724. Offers auctions and sales to members, first day cover expertizing, slide programs for loan, and local chapters. *First Days* is their award-winning large publication which comes eight times a year. $12 annual dues.

3. American Philatelic Society (APS), P.O. Box 8000, State College, PA 16803. Largest stamp collector organization in the United States. Organized 1886. Over 50,000 members. Sales circuits, stamp insurance, recognized expertizing service, quality handbooks, member research library, translation service, exhibition awards. Business and character references necessary on membership form. Being an APS member in good standing for many years is a good business reference, because the APS has a complaint procedure whereby members may be expelled for unethical business conduct. Ninety-six page monthly journal of

the highest quality, covering basic and detailed philatelic research: *The American Philatelist*. Annual dues are $15 for U.S. addresses, plus a one-time $3 admission fee.

4. American Revenue Association (ARA), 701 South First Avenue 332, Arcadia, CA 91006. Local chapters, sales circuits, handbooks, exhibition awards. For those interested in revenue stamps and related material. *The American Revenuer* is the society journal published ten times per year. Dues are $15 annually.

5. American Topical Association (ATA), Box 630, Johnstown, PA 15907. Has study units (separate societies with their own publications) and official handbooks on most popular topical (thematic) subjects on stamps such as birds, trains, space, sports, scouts, dogs, etc. *Topical Time* is a ninety-plus page journal which comes with the membership fee of $10 per year.

6. Bureau Issues Association (BIA), 834 Devonshire Way, Sunnyvale, CA 94087. Publications, journal, and directory. Serious study organization for U.S. Bureau of Engraving and Printing stamps. Monthly publication *The United States Specialist*. Annual dues $15.

7. Confederate Stamp Alliance (CSA), Box 14, Manitowoc, WI 54220. About 650 members interested in the philately of Civil War period Confederate stamps and covers. Directory, expertizing service for Confederate material, and exhibition awards. *Confederate Philatelist* is their bimonthly journal. Annual dues $18.

8. Errors, Freaks and Oddities Collectors Club (EFOCC), 1903 Village Road West, Norwood, MA 02062. Group which studies production errors of stamps. Sales circuits, expertizing, study groups, exhibition awards. Bimonthly journal *EFO Collector*. Dues $10 per year.

9. Junior Philatelists of America (JPA), Box 8028, State College, PA 16803. Organization for pre-adult collectors. Directory, sales circuits, exhibition awards. Bimonthly journal *Philatelic Observer*. Dues are $6 per year for juniors, $12 for adult supporting members.

10. Precancel Stamp Society (PSS), Box 160, Walkersville, MD 21793. For collectors of precancelled stamps. Sales circuits, local chapters, expertizing, handbooks, exhibition awards. Monthly journal *The Precancel Forum*. Annual dues $10.

11. United Postal Stationery Society (UPSS), 1601 Clair Martin

Place, Ambler, PA 19002. For collectors of postal stationery, namely embossed stamped envelopes and government postal cards (Scott "U" and "UX" numbers). Local chapters, directory, sales circuits, expertizing service, exhibition awards, handbooks. Bimonthly journal *Postal Stationery*. Dues are $12 per year.

12. U.S. Philatelic Classics Society (USPCS), P.O. Box 1011, Falls Church, VA 22041. The most prestigious organization for collectors and students of nineteenth century U.S. stamps. Local chapters, publication, exhibition awards. Seventy-two page quarterly journal called *The Chronicle of the U.S. Classic Postal Issues* is of the highest quality as far as philatelic publications go, containing scholarly articles showing in-depth research of permanent value. Membership in this society is a must for serious collectors and investors of nineteenth century U.S. postage stamps of value. Annual dues $15.

13. War Cover Club (WCC), Box 464, Feasterville, PA 19047. Group which studies covers from all wars in which mail is obtainable by collectors. Local chapters, mail auctions, handbooks, and exhibition awards. *War Cover Bulletin* is the society's official publication. Annual dues $5.

14. Western Cover Society (WCS), 9877 Elmar Avenue, Oakland, CA 94603. Organization devoted to the study of western U.S. nineteenth century mail, especially things like California express covers. Directory and annual convention. Quarterly journal called *Western Express*. Annual dues $15.

15. Writer's Unit #30 (WU, an affiliate of the APS), 2501 Drexel Street, Vienna, VA 22180. Membership open to philatelic writers or those interested in such. Quarterly journal *The Philatelic Communicator*. Annual dues $10.

OTHER SOCIETIES

There are many, many other stamp organizations of more specialized interests, including clubs and societies which study single U.S. states, single foreign countries or regions, and topicals and types of cancellations.

For up-to-date listings of these specialist groups, check the latest issue of *Linn's Stamp News* or *Stamp Collector* (see Chapter 12). Or write to the American Philatelic Society for general society addresses, or to the American Topical Association for thematic groups.

Your local stamp dealer can be found by looking under "Stamps for Collectors" in the Yellow Pages. A local dealer should be able to help you find any nearby stamp club, the hours and days it meets, and how to contact it. Many local clubs meet every two weeks, usually at a rented or donated room in a bank building, library, YMCA, church, etc.

Always remember to include a self-addressed stamped envelope when writing for information to any stamp club or society. Write first to be sure what the latest dues are before sending your dues payment, and to verify the society's mailing address because the location of the corresponding secretary/treasurer sometimes changes when a stamp society elects new officers.

Chapter 12

Stamp Periodicals

Weekly stamp newspapers keep the serious philatelist up to date regarding price changes in stamp market values, recently discovered errors and forgeries, and new issues of the world's postal administrations. There are four major general interest stamp periodicals published in the United States: *Linn's Stamp News*, *Stamp Collector*, *Stamps*, and *The American Philatelist*. Let's look at each of these publications, with an analysis of the advantages and disadvantages of each one.

LINN'S STAMP NEWS The largest circulation stamp periodical in America is *Linn's Stamp News*, P.O. Box 29, Sidney, OH 45365. Subscription price is $28 for one year, $49 for two years. Foreign subscribers must add $40 per year for postage. *Linn's* is published weekly.

At the height of the stamp market boom in the late 1970s and early 1980s, *Linn's* was pushing close to 100,000 subscribers. Present circulation is about 75,000, still a relatively small number when you consider that the U.S. Postal Service estimates that maybe ten million or more U.S. citizens collect stamps.

The number of pages per issue of *Linn's* varies from around eighty to a hundred, depending upon the amount of advertising and whether or not a special issue is being printed for distribution at a prominent stamp show somewhere in the country. Page size is 11 by 17 inches, of normal newspaper-type stock, with sporadic use of colored ink for ads or for illustrating new stamp issues on the cover.

Page three of *Linn's* lists the Table of Contents, which includes regular features like "Collecting First Day Covers," "Stamp Market Tips," and "Postal History." Every week there is an updated section for forthcoming stamp auctions and a calendar of stamp shows to be held in the United States and foreign countries. Also the U.S. and Canadian stamp program for the entire year appears in a corrected version each week; the timetables and denominations of new issues are often changed for projected new stamps, and a first day cover collector needs to know when to order new stamps on cover, and how much to send to pay for their face values.

One of the best parts of *Linn's Stamp News* is the weekly "Trends of Stamp Values" section which lists the current retail market prices of the mint, unused (never cancelled but without gum), and used stamps of a few selected countries. Also a plus sign (+) after the "Trends" value indicates that the stamp has increased in price since it was last listed in *Linn's*, while a minus sign (-) shows that the market value has decreased since that country's stamps were last listed. Several years might pass between *Linn's* "Trends" listing for an average country, while extremely popular nations like the United States appear more frequently. "Trends" identifies stamps by Scott numbers.

The "Readers' Opinions" page of *Linn's* prints letters to the editors from readers, averaging about eight to twelve letters per issue. Letters indicate concerns of stamp collectors and investors, and often famous collectors and dealers write strong opinions on controversial topics such as a fair price spread between wholesale and retail stamp prices, or how much a collector should pay for never-hinged original gum on a stamp.

Display ads throughout the paper, and a dozen or more pages of fine print classified ads at the back make *Linn's* a gold mine of current stamp prices. Dealers often advertise their specific buying or selling prices for individual stamps. Anyone can place a classified ad in the paper; rates start at $5.60 for up to twenty-five words inserted in one issue.

Linn's is essential for serious collectors and dealers. The latest information about new stamp discoveries, stamp fraud arrests and convictions, and upcoming major auctions are alone worth the price of a year's subscription.

STAMP COLLECTOR   Second in circulation among the philatelic weeklies, with about half of the number of *Linn's* subscribers, is *Stamp Collector*, P.O. Box 10, Albany, OR 97321. Subscription price is $23.94 for one year, $39.88 for two years. Collectors in foreign countries can get it by surface mail for $13 extra per year, but air mail delivery is substantially higher.

Stamp Collector is a professionally written, but friendly and easy to read paper with something of interest to collectors from beginners to advanced philatelists. Regular weekly features include an auction calendar, letters to the editor, foreign exchange rate tables, stamp society information, and a list of leading stamp stores around the country.

The number of pages per issue varies a lot, from thirty-six to forty for an average copy to many more pages for special issues printed for major stamp exhibitions. The classified ads occupy a half dozen pages at the rear of the newspaper, and the "Classified Index" is especially helpful for quickly finding a particular classified for the kind of material that you wish to buy or sell.

Stamp Collector page size runs 11-1/4 inches wide by 14-3/4 inches high of normal newsprint stock. Colored ink is used liberally, often with quite accurate representation of the actual colors of the stamps depicted.

True, *Stamp Collector* has fewer pages than *Linn's*, and some advertisers use only one of these publications, but *Stamp Collector* is cheaper for a subscription, and provides all of the new issue information for upcoming U.S. and Canadian issues that *Linn's* does, as well as similar show and auction data.

Linn's might be compared to a big city newspaper, while *Stamp Collector* more closely resembles a local town journal. A general collector or stamp investor can get along with either one of these periodicals, but anyone who insists on being thoroughly informed on happenings in the stamp world should subscribe to both.

Information supplied by the publishers, based on their own surveys, shows that some people subscribe to one, while many just get *Linn's* or *Stamp Collector* alone, so we can't make a definitive statement as to what kind of philatelist reads either publication. *Stamp Collector*'s staff has statistics that say that their readers have an above average income.

STAMPS *Stamps* magazine is printed on newspaper stock. *Stamps* is published weekly at 85 Canisteo Street, Hornell, NY 14843. Subscription price is $22.00 per year in the United States and Canada for second class mail rate, $44.00 for foreign countries.

Page size of *Stamps* is 11 inches wide by 14 inches high. Color is used mostly for advertising on the outside and inside covers and at selected places within the magazine. The number of pages per issue varies quite a bit, from fifty-six for a smaller copy to 144 for a typical special issue.

Stamps has improved its image lately by incorporating new columnists and articles of more substantial interest, as opposed to the short and relatively simple articles that were characteristic of the magazine in the 1970s. There are plenty of display ads in *Stamps*, with merchandise for sale ranging from beginner's first day covers to great rarities. Some collectors subscribe to *Stamps* only for the ads.

Linn's and *Stamp Collector* tend to have articles that are more lengthy and in-depth than those in *Stamps*. But the classified ads at the back of *Stamps* are the easiest to read, with bold print and some space between each ad so you don't get dizzy trying to find an ad of interest.

Regular departments featured in *Stamps* are letters to the editor, "U.S. Classics," "The Error Scene," "Cachet Briefs" (upcoming special events covers), "New Issues and Discoveries," and "Stamp Market Tips."

Circulation of *Stamps* has been down somewhat in recent years, and trails *Stamp Collector* by several thousand.

For a dollar bill any of the publishers of *Linn's Stamp News, Stamp Collector,* or *Stamps* will be happy to send you a sample copy of their periodicals. Look them all over and then decide for yourself which you prefer as a subscription in your plan to be an informed philatelist. And if you intend to be a serious investor or stamp dealer, you need all three so you don't miss anything.

THE AMERICAN PHILATELIST

The official monthly journal of the American Philatelic Society (mentioned in Chapter 11) is *The American Philatelist*, an extremely high quality publication in magazine format, printed on slick paper with professional printing results. Subscription is included as part of membership in the APS: $18 United States, $21 Canada, and $24 for other foreign countries, which includes the admission fee and yearly membership fee.

Normal sized issues of *The American Philatelist* run to ninety-six pages of 8-1/2 inches by 11 inches. Good black and white photographs illustrate the articles; color is sometimes used with striking effect to show a series of rare stamps or covers in their natural shades.

Monthly columns and departments include an extensive and high class letters to the editor section in which current philatelic topics are debated intelligently, "Literature in Review," "Insurance Information," "Postal History Notes," exhibition data, and a calendar of upcoming shows and U.S. new issues.

The articles in *The American Philatelist* are often technical, very detailed studies of particular stamps or postal history topics, and may at first glance seem to be of only marginal interest to the general stamp collector. But many collectors learn a lot of useful information from reading such articles, including acquiring knowledge of forgery detection, how to identify papers and gums, and tips on paper preservation and storage.

An average of five pages of selected classified ads can be found in the back of each month's issue, and an index of display advertisers is quite helpful in locating the ads of favorite dealers.

Each issue has a list of new APS members, along with the names and addresses of members who have been expelled from the society for misconduct in their stamp business dealings. It is worth the subscription price of *The American Philatelist* to keep up to date on unethical individuals who could someday defraud you of a large amount of stamp money.

You might say that *The American Philatelist* is to stamp collecting as *National Geographic* is to world travel, or as *Scientific American* is to science. Not all of *The American Philatelist's* articles are easy to comprehend, and many of them wouldn't make good late night reading for light entertainment.

But if it is in *The American Philatelist* it has a good chance of being an article of lasting value, often the result of years of research and study by a philatelic specialist who is recording his findings for the first time in formal publication.

A sample copy of *The American Philatelist* can be obtained by mailing two dollars to the American Philatelic Society, P.O. Box 8000, State College, PA 16803, and asking for the Society's journal.

Chapter 13

Postal Administrations

Buying stamps directly from a government's postal administration is fun and informative. You get new issues at face value, first day covers on time, and often brochures describing upcoming stamps. You can send a deposit and have a standing order to get one or more sets of all new issues as they are released so you don't miss anything.

Although you'll be paying just face value for mint stamps and therefore avoid a dealer's commission, the postage and handling charges on small orders may make it unprofitable to buy a few stamps directly from a foreign postal authority, when compared to buying a couple of new stamps from a local dealer who buys in large quantities and can afford to resell at a small premium.

First, decide what countries you want to collect. Then see if you can get new issues cheaply from a local stamp shop. Finally, if the excitement and cost of ordering directly make sense to you, then try a sample order to a postal administration and wait for your stamps to arrive in the mail!

UNITED STATES POSTAL SERVICE

The U.S. Postal Service is the postal system in the United States. Organized in 1971 from the old U.S. Post Office Department, the Postal Service is described as an independent quasi-governmental agency which makes its own decisions via its Board of Governors who are appointed by the President of the United States with U.S. Senate confirmation.

The Philatelic Sales Division is a branch of the Postal Service, operating over the counter and mail order service expressly for stamp collectors.

Current stamps may by purchased at the sales windows of the U.S. Philatelic Center, 475 L'Enfant Plaza West, S.W., Washington, DC, Monday through Saturday from 9:00 A.M. to 5:00 P.M. or by mail from:

U.S. Postal Service
Philatelic Sales Division
Washington, DC 20265

By sending a postal card or letter requesting to be placed on the "Philatelic Catalog" mailing list, you will receive every two months a color-illustrated, multi-page price list of all current U.S. stamps for sale at face value plus a small handling fee (50 cents for up to 500 stamps, $1.50 for 3,000 stamps, etc.).

The U.S. Postal Service's Philatelic Sales Division supplies mint commemorative and regular issue stamps, coils, booklets, penalty official stamps, embossed envelopes and postal cards, aerogrammes, duck hunting stamps, air mails, precancels, and postage dues, all at face value from selected stock on hand.

In addition, the Sales Division catalog lists stamp guidebooks for sale, mint sets by the year, souvenir cards and folders, simple stamp collecting kits (twenty page album for beginners, stamps, hinges, and a descriptive booklet), maximum cards, exhibition cards, and stamp art prints.

The U.S. Postal Service cancels first day covers at the city of issue or regional centers which vary for different stamps. See Chapter 5 for how to prepare first day covers. The Sales Division has a ten dollar minimum order for mail sales.

UNITED NATIONS POSTAL ADMINISTRATION

The United Nations Postal Administration supplies mint stamps and first day covers of United Nations stamps which can only be postally used at a United Nations postal facility in New York City, Geneva (Switzerland), or Vienna (Austria); different issues in the appropriate currency of those three locations.

An order form for purchasing stamps from the United Nations may be obtained by writing to:

United Nations Postal Administration
P.O. Box 5900
Grand Central Station
New York, NY 10017

There is a fifty cent service charge on United Nations stamp orders under two dollars, and the customer must pay return postage on orders. United Nations stamps were started in 1951, and except for the tenth anniversary souvenir sheet (Scott UN #38) costing well over $100, all back issues of United Nations stamps can be bought for reasonable prices from dealers, allowing the new collector to have hope of completing a United Nations "country" collection on a modest budget.

CANADA
POST CORPORATION

Probably the most popular country collected by U.S. collectors, after U.S. stamps and United Nations material, is Canada. The Canada Post Corporation is the official postal service agency in Canada, and the philatelic wing of it has a mailing address as follows:

> Philatelic Service
> National Philatelic Center
> Canada Post Corporation
> Antigonish, Nova Scotia B2G 2R8
> Canada

They charge fifty cents handling on orders under five dollars, and will service collector-prepared first day covers for fifteen cents per cover. Write to Canada Post for their latest list of stamps available if you are interested in buying the latest Canadian issues by mail.

WESTERN EUROPEAN
POSTAL AGENCIES

Space limitations prohibit listing all postal administrations of the world, but some of the more popular countries to collect are those of western Europe listed below. Write to any that interest you and ask for a price list and ordering instructions for current stamps. If you write in English, you should still get a response. Be patient: air mail and government postal bureaucracies are notoriously slow even in the late twentieth century!

1. Austria
   Oesterreichische Post
   Briefmarkenversandstelle
   A-1011 Vienna, Austria

2. Belgium
   Regie des Postes
   Service des Collectionneurs
   1000 Brussels, Belgium

3. Denmark
   Postens Filateli
   Raadhuspladsen 59
   DK-1550 Copenhagen V,
   Denmark

4. Finland
   Philatelic Section
   G.D. of Posts and Telecommuni-
   cations
   P.O. Box 654
   SF-00101 Helsinki 10, Finland

5.	France	Service Philatelique 61-63 Rue de Douai 75436 Paris Cedex 09, France
6.	Germany	Versandstelle fur Postwert- zeichen Postfach 20 00 6000 Frankfurt 1, West Ger- many
7.	Great Britain	Philatelic Bureau British Post Office 20 Brandon Street Edinburgh EH3 5TT Scotland Great Britain
8.	Greece	Philatelic Service Greek Post Office 100 Aiolou Street Athens 131, Greece
9.	Ireland	Philatelic Bureau GPO Dublin 1, Ireland
10.	Italy	Ufficio Principale Filatelico Via Maria de Fiori, 103/A 00187 Rome, Italy
11.	Liechtenstein	Philatelic Service FL-9490 Vaduz Liechtenstein
12.	Luxembourg	Direction des Postes Office des Timbres L-2020 Luxembourg Luxembourg
13.	Monaco	Office des Emissions de Timbres-Poste Principalite de Monaco
14.	Netherlands	Philatelic Service Post Office P.O. Box 30051 9700-RN Groningen The Netherlands

15. Norway   Postens Filatelitjeneste
Postboks 1085 Sentrum
Oslo 1, Norway

16. Portugal   Philatelic Office
Av. Casal Ribeiro 28-2
1096 Lisbon Codex, Portugal

17. San Marino   Philatelic Office
47031 Republic of San Marino

18. Spain   Servicio Filatelico Internacional
Direccion General de Correos
Madrid 14, Spain

19. Sweden   PFA Postens Frimarksavdelning
S-105 02 Stockholm, Sweden

20. Switzerland   Philatelic Service PTT
Zeughausgasse 19
CH-3030 Bern, Switzerland

OTHER COUNTRIES   Besides the list of western European postal agencies above, here are some nations whose stamps enjoy popularity among United States collectors.

1. Australia   Philatelic Bureau
GPO Box 9988
Melbourne, Victoria 3001
Australia

2. Israel   Philatelic Service
Ministry of Communications
Tel Aviv-Yafo 61 080, Israel

3. Japan   Philatelic Section
CPO Box 888
Tokyo 100-91, Japan

4. Mexico   Departamento Filatelico
Edificio de Correos
2 Piso, Tacuba 1
06000 Mexico 1, D.F., Mexico

5. New Zealand   Philatelic Bureau
Post Office, Private Bag
Wanganui, New Zealand

6. Philippines   Philatelic Division
Bureau of Posts
Manila, Philippines

7. South Africa   Philatelic Services
GPO
Pretoria 0001, South Africa

8. Vatican City   Ufficio Filatelico
Governatorato, Vatican City

STILL OTHER POSTAL AGENCIES   World postal administrations not listed here may be found periodically in the philatelic weeklies (Chapter 12) or by consulting *Linn's World Stamp Almanac* published by Amos Press, P.O. Box 29, Sidney, OH 45367.

Chapter 14

Some Famous Stamps

Fame is fragile, unpredictable, too frequently short-lived. Through the lens of time we distort and romanticize the past. With fads and flourishes we worship and glamorize the present. With naive hope we long for the glories and mysteries of the future.

Stamps get famous for the same reasons that people do: they have interesting stories with universal appeal, they show human nature at its best or worst, and they focus our attention on the elements of chance and choice which govern the events in the lives of individuals and nations.

Here are a few famous stamps and their stories, or at least what can be told of them in the space devoted to this chapter.

THE ONE CENT BRITISH GUIANA

The One Cent British Guiana Black on Magenta stamp of 1856 (Scott #13) is the most valuable stamp in the world. One copy is known, last sold at the Robert A. Siegel Auction Galleries in New York City in 1980, hammer price $935,000 (including the auctioneer's fee).

The British Guiana is currently unpriced in Scott's catalog, and who knows what it will bring when it is sold again?

Found by a schoolboy who was searching through some correspondence in 1872, looking for stamps for his collection, this king of stamp rarities has passed through a number of different hands to its present anonymous owner. Count Ferrari once owned it. So did Arthur Hind who bid $30,000 for it at public auction after Ferrari's collection was put up for sale between the two World Wars. Ferrari had paid only about 150 British pounds for it when he bought it from a Liverpool dealer!

Around 1939 Frederick Small bought it for about $50,000, and held it anonymously until it was sold again in 1970 for $240,000 to a conglomerate of Pennsylvania investors. They sold it in 1980 for $935,000 to another unknown buyer.

There is a story of Arthur Hind buying a second copy of the

British Guiana, and then immediately burning it with his cigar in front of the horrified seller, in order to keep his the only copy in the world. This is probably a myth. Only one copy has ever been verified, and no British Empire collection (including the fabulous Royal Collection in England) is complete without it.

THE TWENTY-FOUR CENT AIR MAIL INVERT

People who know nothing about stamp collecting have often heard of this famous stamp (Scott #C3a, catalog value $120,000).

In May 1918, a young stockbroker's clerk named William T. Robey walked into a Washington, DC post office and bought a pane (sheet) of the new twenty-four cent air mail stamp showing an airplane in flight. Robey paid $24 cash to the window clerk for a 100 stamp face value sheet. But when he picked it up he noticed that the airplanes were flying upside down, and later described his feelings at that moment: "My heart stood still."

The window clerk tried to get it back from him, but Robey refused and left the post office with his newly purchased treasure. Two postal inspectors quickly visited Robey at his home, but they couldn't convince him to part with the inverts.

Robey later sold the sheet to Philadelphia stamp dealer Eugene Klein for $15,000 (original cost $24). Klein sold it to Colonel Ned Green for $20,000. Colonel Green was the son of the wealthy financier Hetty Green. He was known for his eccentricity, money, and love of stamps. Green lightly numbered each stamp on the sheet on its back with a pencil, and he broke up the pane into blocks and singles which he eventually sold off.

It is probably not true that somebody's wife used the famous air mail inverts on social letters. Or that some of them were accidentally sucked by a vacuum cleaner or blown off the owner's stamp table into a waste basket which the maid emptied in the trash bin. Theoretically three additional panes should exist because they were printed with this known pane, but they have never surfaced and were presumably destroyed before being released to the public.

Most of the original pane of 100 stamps has been accounted for, including several position blocks owned on and off by the Weill brothers, famous stamp dealers still in business on Royal Street in New Orleans.

THE POST OFFICE
MAURITIUS ISSUES

The Post Office Mauritius stamps are among the fabulous rarities of philately. Only a few copies are known today, including a couple of covers. I couldn't resist telling their story in Chapter 1, so turn there and read it if you haven't yet!

THE
HAWAIIAN MISSIONARIES

The Hawaiian Missionaries of 1851-52 were mostly used by American missionaries living in Hawaii. These first four stamps listed under Hawaii in the Scott catalog (values range from $9000 for the cheapest variety to $350,000 for the mint two cent blue) have long been popular among collectors of stamp rarities. All known off-cover copies are more or less damaged, but their high market price is due to tremendous demand.

In 1892 a French stamp collector, Gaston Leroux, was murdered by a fellow collector, Hector Giroux. The police were at first confused because there was no sign of anything missing from Monsieur Leroux's Paris apartment until it was discovered that the two cent Hawaiian missionary stamp wasn't in his collection.

Giroux was arrested and confessed to the crime. The astonishing thing was that Giroux could afford to buy the stamp but Leroux wouldn't sell it. Such is the extreme to which serious philatelists will go to obtain a needed stamp for their album!

The Hawaiian missionaries come on the market from time to time, always at steep prices. Famous collectors who have owned them are Count Ferrari, Alfred Caspary, and Maurice Burrus.

U.S. POSTMASTER
PROVISIONALS

Before the introduction of regular U.S. government postage stamps in 1847, local postmasters issued their own provisional stamps in certain cities. All are rare today, and some are unique, only one copy known, such as the 1846 Boscawen, New Hampshire five cent blue (catalog value $60,000 on cover) and the 1846 Lockport, New York five cent red (catalog value $60,000 on cover).

Other famous U.S. Postmaster Provisionals are: Alexandria, Virginia ($85,000 on cover), Annapolis, Maryland ($45,000), Baltimore, Maryland — the Postmaster Buchanan issue ($40,000 for the most expensive variety), Millbury, Massachusetts ($50,000), New Haven, Connecticut ($32,000 for the costliest), and the

Saint Louis "Bears" ($40,000 for the most expensive cover). All the above values are from the Scott *Specialized* catalog.

OTHER UNIQUE RARITIES

Other stamps that are known by only one example are the orange color error of the Swedish three skilling 1855 issue (unpriced in current Scott's), the three pence Canadian Postmaster's Provisional of New Carlisle, Quebec of 1851 (unlisted in Scott), and the one cent blue "Z-Grill" U.S. regular issue of 1867 (Scott #85a) which is often called the rarest U.S. stamp. This one cent Z-Grill is the only copy available to collectors, the other one being locked up in the Miller Collection of the New York Public Library. The available Z-Grill copy was auctioned off by Superior Stamp & Coin Company of Beverly Hills, CA as Lot #186 of their November 10, 1986 Dr. Jerry Buss Sale. The final bid was $380,000 plus a ten percent auction commission for a total of $418,000 paid for the most expensive U.S. stamp ever auctioned!

Glossary

This is a glossary of the most common stamp terms and their recognized abbreviations as used in the standard catalogs, dealer price lists, auction descriptions, and at stamp exhibitions.

ADHESIVE: A postage stamp, with or without its original gum.

AMERICAN PHILATELIC SOCIETY (APS): Largest stamp collector organization in the United States. Issues expertizing certificates.

AMERICAN STAMP DEALER'S ASSOCIATION (ASDA): The largest and best known stamp dealer's organization in the United States. Being an ASDA member helps verify a dealer's integrity.

APPROVALS: Stamps sent by mail from companies to collectors who choose the ones they wish to keep, and return the balance with their payment for items retained.

AS IS: A sales term meaning that the lot cannot be returned for a refund once it is bought and taken home. Usually refers to defective stamps.

AVERAGE (AV or AVE or AVG): Lower grade stamps, generally not of investment or exhibition quality.

BACK OF BOOK (BOB): Section of the standard catalog after the regular issues and commemoratives. Includes special deliveries, postage dues, revenues, etc.

BACKSTAMPED (B/S): Handstamped postal marking on the back of a cover.

BISECT: Stamp cut in half and cancelled on a cover. Used to pay half the postage value of the original uncut stamp.

BLIND PERF: Perforation holes not punched out, but impressions of the hole puncher are evident. Not imperforate or of the market value of true imperforates.

BLOCK (BLK or ⊞ or ☐): Four or more stamps still joined together in block form. Unless stated otherwise, refers to block-of-four.

BOURSE: Place where dealers meet to buy and sell stamps to the public. Also called a stamp show.

BRITISH NORTH AMERICA (BNA): Stamps of Canada and its former independent stamp-issuing provinces.

BRITISH PHILATELIC ASSOCIATION (BPA): Great Britain stamp society. Issues expertizing certificates.

BULL'S EYE: Cancel which is centered more or less wholly on a stamp. Also called "socked-on-the-nose" (SOTN or SON).

CACHET: A printed design on the left front of a cover, placed there for philatelic purposes; often a first day cover.

CANCELLED TO ORDER (CTO): Stamps which never saw postal use, but instead are mass cancelled in full panes by a country interested in selling them at a discount to collectors for revenue.

CATALOG VALUE (CV or C/V or CAT VAL): Price quote for a stamp in a standard philatelic catalog.

CENSORED: Cover which has been handstamped to indicate that it has been read by a censor; usually military mail.

CENTERING: How well a stamp's design is centered relative to the unprinted margin between the design and perforations or stamp's edge. Off center stamps are so described, for example, centered to top (CTT) or centered to bottom (CTB).

CHANGELING: A stamp whose color has been chemically changed since it left the post office where it was sold.

CINDERELLA: A paper label which is not a postage stamp, although it often appears to be. Not necessarily meant to defraud; may be a fantasy issue of a nonexistent country or a privately-produced adhesive for business purposes, etc.

CIRCULAR DATE STAMP (CDS): A circular cancel which has the date appearing inside.

CLASSIC: A stamp issued over a century ago. Old, rare, and valuable stamps.

COIL: Stamps issued in roll form, with two opposite edges being straight.

COLLATERAL: Material related to stamps, such as route maps, Postmaster General autographs, post office photos, etc. Often used to enhance a philatelic exhibit.

COLOR SHIFT: Misalignment of colors, a production error on a multicolored stamp.

COMMEMORATIVE (COMMEM): A stamp issued for a limited time period to honor a person, place, or thing. Not a regular or definitive issue.

CORNER CARD: Return address portion of an envelope; often referring to that area on nineteenth century covers.

COVER (CVR or ⊠): An envelope designed for postal use.

CREASE (CR): A permanent fold on a stamp or cover. Mentioned in auction descriptions as a warning because creases lower a stamp's value.

CUT CANCEL (CC): A cancellation which cuts through the stamp. Usually drastically reduces the value.

CUT SQUARE: The printed stamp area of an embossed envelope, cut away from the rest of the cover.

CUT TO SHAPE (CTS): A stamp, usually imperforate, which has had its margins cut to border the printed design. Usually reduces the value when compared with one not cut to shape.

DEAD COUNTRY: A nonexistent nation or political entity which once issued its own stamps but no longer does.

DEFINITIVE: Regular postal issue, on sale for a long time at post offices. Not a commemorative.

DISTURBED GUM (DG): Damaged stamp gum.

ENTIRE: Full piece of postal stationery (as opposed to a cut square).

ERROR, FREAK, ODDITY (EFO): Category of stamps which are errors.

ESSAY (E): A proposed stamp design, often in stamp form. Should not be the finally accepted design or it would then be known as a proof.

ESTIMATED (EST): Estimated net value, a predicted auction price.

EX: An auction term meaning from a famous collection; for example, EX-Ashbrook. Gives a philatelic item more prestige and possibly more value due to its provenance.

EXPLODED: A post office booklet of stamps which has been broken apart into its component panes, covers, etc.

EXTREMELY FINE (EF or XF): A stamp grade meaning high quality; just below the grade of Superb.

FAULTS (FLTS): With damage.

FIELD POST OFFICE (FPO): A military postal facility in the theater of conflict. Could also be an army post office (APO).

FINE (F): A stamp grade meaning minimally acceptable quality, above Very Good but below Very Fine. Perforations usually clear of the design.

FIRST DAY COVER (FDC): An envelope with a stamp cancelled on its first day of issue.

FIRST FLIGHT COVER (FFC): An envelope flown on the first day of an air mail route.

FISCAL: Revenue use of a stamp; often pen cancelled, usually reducing its value from non-fiscal or regular postal use.

FOLDED LETTER (FL): A letter folded and sent without an envelope.

FRAME: The printed border of a stamp's design, between the vignette in the center and the edge of the stamp's paper.

FRANKED: The postage used to pay a letter; for example, franked with two stamps. Free franks have no stamps attached.

FRONT: The stamped and addressed side of a cover; when used alone it refers to just the front of an envelope remaining. Usually reduces the value compared to a full intact envelope.

FUGITIVE INK: Ink used in stamp printing that dissolves in water.

GRILL: Little impressions in stamp paper to let the cancel's ink soak in to prevent reuse of the stamp. Prevalent on certain nineteenth century U.S. stamps.

GUM: The adhesive glue on the back of a stamp.

GUTTER PAIR (G/PR): Two stamps separated by a piece of unprinted paper, as a result of production processes.

HANDSTAMPED (HS or H/S): Cancelled with a handstamping device.

HEAVILY CANCELLED (HC): Abnormally dense cancel ink on a stamp; greatly reduces a used stamp's value.

HEAVILY HINGED (HH): A stamp with hinge paper adhering in distracting amounts. Reduces value from lightly hinged.

HIGHWAY POST OFFICE (HPO): A mobile post office located in a truck.

HINGED (H): Showing evidence of having been hinged (as opposed to mint, never hinged).

HINGE REMNANTS (HR): Pieces of hinge adhering to a stamp.

IMPERFORATE (IMPERF): Stamps issued without perforations.

INVERTED (INVT): Error in which part of a stamp's design appears abnormally upside down.

LEFT, RIGHT (L, R): Auction descriptions used in abbreviations: CTL (centered to left).

LIGHTLY CANCELLED (LC): Pleasingly light cancel on a stamp; usually enhances its value.

LIGHTLY HINGED (LH): Just a trace of gum disturbance where a hinge once was on a stamp.

LINE PAIR (LP or L/P): A guideline copy of a pair of adjacent coil stamps. Used to help guarantee the coil nature of the stamps.

LOCAL: Limited geographical use, such as stamps made for use in one city.

LOWER LEFT/LOWER RIGHT (LL/LR): Positions on single stamps or blocks.

MANUSCRIPT (MS): Another name for pen cancellation.

MARGIN (MRGN): The unprinted area between the outside of a stamp's design and the edge of the paper.

MARGINAL INSCRIPTION (MI): Printed information in the attached selvage around a stamp.

MINOR DEFECT (MD): Small damaged area of a stamp. Beware of advertised minor defects turning out to be major when they are purchased!

MINT (M or *): An unused stamp with gum if issued as such.

MINT, NEVER HINGED (MNH or **): The gum on a stamp is undisturbed by hinging or other means.

MISPERFORATED (MISPERF): Perforations out of alignment instead of being in their usual place between stamp designs.

MULTIPLE: More than one of the same stamp still attached to each other as issued (with or without perforations).

NEVER HINGED (NH or **): Gum which shows no evidence of ever having been hinged.

NO GUM (NG): A stamp without any gum on the back, usually referring to one which once had gum. Another name for a no gum stamp is *unused* (as opposed to *mint* which means with gum).

OBSOLETE: Stamps which are no longer for sale in post offices.

OFF CENTER: A stamp whose design is significantly not centered on the paper.

OFF PAPER: Used stamps which have been soaked off of or otherwise removed from their envelopes.

ORIGINAL GUM (OG): The gum as issued is still on the back of a stamp. May or may not be hinged. If original gum, never hinged, it is designated OGNH.

OVERPRINT (OVPT): Official inked impression that has been added to a stamp's design after it was first printed. Overprints may be words or face value changes.

PAIR (PR): Two adjacent stamps still joined together as issued.

PANE: What non-philatelists call a "sheet," the form in which stamps are sold in the post office; the largest flat connected group of stamps that a postal patron can buy.

PERFORATED INITIALS (PERFINS or PI's): Little holes in the configuration of alphabet letters which are punched into stamps as a security, anti-theft measure. Used by businesses and stamp-issuing governments.

PERFORATION (PERF): One of the holes punched between stamps to facilitate separation.

PHILATELIC FOUNDATION CERTIFICATE (PFC):   An expertizing document that accompanies stamps certified as genuine by the prestigious Philatelic Foundation of New York City.

PHILATELIC TRADER'S SOCIETY (PTS): A London-based organization of worldwide stamp dealers. A PTS logo displayed in a dealer's ad helps verify his integrity.

PHILATELIC USE: A cover which was prepared and mailed by a philatelist. Also called *controlled mail*. The opposite of unplanned commercial mail.

PHILATELY: Stamp collecting. Literally, "love of exemption from taxation" from the Greek words *philos* (love) and *ateleia* (exempt from tax), referring to postage being prepaid by a stamp. Technically, philately means the serious study of stamps, not just accumulating them.

PLATE BLOCK (PB): A number or inscription block, usually of four stamps. Also called plate number block (PNB).

PLATE NUMBER (PL NO or PL #): The control production number imprinted on the selvage attached to a stamp.

POST CARD (PC or P/C): A picture card sold to tourists for mailing. Don't confuse with *postal card*.

POSTAGE DUE (PD): Mail sent without enough postage. Also refers to special stamps issued to collect insufficient postage on undelivered mail.

POSTAL CARD (PC or P/C also): A government-issued card that you buy at a post office, blank on the back, and printed with a stamp on the front upper right-hand corner.

POSTAL HISTORY: The study of mail service. Also refers to covers as a synonym.

POSTAL STATIONERY: Embossed stamped envelopes and postal cards.

POSTMARK (PMK): A marking on mail to indicate date mailed, routes travelled, amount of postage paid, etc. May be stamped with a preformed device or handwritten.

POST OFFICE DEPARTMENT (POD): What the U.S. Postal Service was called prior to 1971.

PRECANCEL (PREC): A stamp that has been cancelled prior to being stuck on a piece of mail.

PROOF (P or PR or PRF): A trial impression of a stamp in its design as finally issued, either in black ink or in the color of issues. Don't confuse with essays.

RAILWAY POST OFFICE (RPO): A postal station on board a railway car.

REGUMMED (RG): An unused stamp that has had faked gum applied after its original gum washed off.

REPRINT (R): A stamp made from the original equipment long after the first issue of it became obsolete.

ROULETTE (R): A method of separating stamps by slits in the paper instead of perforations.

SCOTT CATALOG VALUE (SCV): The price of a stamp quoted in the official Scott Catalog.

SELVAGE (SEL or SELV): The paper (either printed or blank) that is attached outside of the stamps on a pane. Also spelled selvege or selvedge.

SEMI-POSTAL: A stamp issued for a charity purpose, with two values imprinted on it; one for payment of postage and one for donation to charity. Listed under "B" numbers in the Scott catalogs.

SEPARATION (SEP): Stamps separated (usually partially) at their natural perforations.

SET: A complete group of stamps of similar designs, as issued. Designated by catalog numbers like: 75-83; as opposed to an incomplete set with some stamps missing, shown by a diagonal line between the end values: 75/83.

SE-TENANT: Stamps of different designs attached adjacently to each other as issued.

SHEET: The complete piece of paper of stamps as originally printed. Often broken into two or four panes for post office sale. When non-philatelists say they bought a *sheet* of post office stamps, they really mean that they bought a *pane*.

SHORT PERFORATION (SH PF): A perforation "tooth" pulled off of a stamp.

SLEEPER: A stamp that is undervalued in the catalogs or marketplace. Unrecognized underpriced items.

SOUVENIR SHEET (SS or S/S): A small pane of one or more stamps, issued for commemorative purposes by a postal government, often specifically for collectors.

SPACE FILLER: A badly damaged, expensive stamp that takes the place of the extremely valuable, sound copy which the collector cannot afford.

SPECIMEN (S): A stamp overprinted with a number or the word "Specimen" for distribution to governments or other authorities to serve as a sample of a newly-issued stamp.

STAMPLESS COVER: An envelope that went through the mails without adhesive stamps on it. Usually refers to pre-Civil War mail before adhesive stamps became widespread.

STRAIGHT EDGE (SE or S/E): A stamp with a natural or cut straight edge, although originally issued as perforated in most cases.

SUPERB (SUP or S): The top grade for stamps. Essentially perfectly centered with no defects. Used recklessly by liberal graders; very few old stamps are technically superb.

SURCHARGE: An overprint on a stamp that changes its face value.

TEAR (TR): A rip in a stamp. Used as an auction description. Enormously decreases a stamp's value in most cases.

TETE-BECHE: Adjacent stamps from the same pane where one design is upside down in relation to the other.

THIN (TH): A thinned area of a stamp; reduces its value.

TIED ON: A stamp on a cover with the cancel covering both the stamp and cover's paper; helps to insure that the stamp was in fact used on that cover.

TIED TO PIECE (TTP or ▲): A stamp cancelled on a small piece of the original envelope, with the cancel tying on the stamp.

TINY (T): An auction description, for example, tiny thin (TTH), tiny crease (TCR).

TOP/BOTTOM (T/B): Auction description, for example, a top block: T ⊞. Refers to positions.

TOPICALS: Stamps picturing a certain subject, like animals, sports, airplanes. Also called *thematics*.

UNITED STATES POSTAL SERVICE (USPS): Our present postal service, so-called since 1971 when it replaced the old Post Office Department.

UNLISTED (UNL): Not listed in the standard catalogs.

UNUSED (UN): Never cancelled. Technically a stamp that has never been cancelled, but has also lost its original gum. Used as a sloppy definition for mint sometimes.

UPPER LEFT/UPPER RIGHT (UL/UR): Positions on single stamps or blocks.

USED (U or ⊙ or ●): A cancelled stamp.

VARIETY (VAR): A subtype of a basic catalog numbered stamp. For example, color or perforation varieties.

VERY FINE (VF): A high grade stamp, better than fine but less nice than extremely fine. Very fine stamps are usually great for discriminating collectors and investors.

VERY GOOD (VG): An inferior stamp grade, below fine. Very good stamps usually have damaged perforations or the design is cut by the perforations.

VERY LIGHTLY HINGED (VLH): The most delicately imaginable evidence of a trace of gum disturbance where a hinge once was.

VIGNETTE: The main picture or central design of a stamp.

WALLPAPER: A derogatory term meaning unnecessary stamps sold by unscrupulous governments to get money from collectors. Synonymous with sand dunes, black blot, or Communist bloc issues.

WATERMARK (WMK): A slightly thinned area of a stamp that is impressed on it at the time of manufacture of the stamp's paper, as a security measure against counterfeiting.

WITH/WITHOUT (W and W/O): Auction abbreviations. For example, without gum: W/O G.

Index